MW01294209

LIMA

TRAVEL GUIDE

Insider Advice from Expats in Peru

Colin Post and David Lee

Copyright © 2016
Colin Post
All rights reserved

Second edition, revised and updated

Published by Expat Chronicles Media
contact@expat-chronicles.com

Cover design by Oded Sonsino
Edited by Charles Avery

This book or any portion thereof may not be reproduced or used in any manner whatsoever without the express written permission of the author, except for the use of brief quotations in a book review.

Although the author has made every reasonable attempt to provide accurate information, he assumes no responsibility for errors or omissions.

ISBN: 1520420554
ISBN-13: 9781520420554

INTRODUCTION

Lima, located midway down Peru's Pacific coast, has drawn visitors from around the world for centuries. In recent decades, the Machu Picchu ruins have surpassed the capital in attracting more visitors to Peru. Those tourists are fortunate to pass through this great South American capital, the City of Kings. Whether you're looking for art and culture, history, gastronomy, partying or sightseeing, Lima will dazzle and amaze.

Colin had lived in Arequipa, in the south of Peru, for one year when he decided to move to Bogota, Colombia. He scheduled a week to see Lima before his move. By the end of that week, he didn't want to leave. He fell in love with the Moorish architecture, the Green Coast and the humidity that reminded him of home. In Bogota, Colin wondered if he made a mistake. He eventually returned to Lima, where he now lives with his wife and children.

David arrived in Lima during an overland trip through South America in 2011. The food stole his heart (or stomach). He stayed in Lima for the next year, where he delved into the nightlife scene, made new friends and visited the beaches south of the city. While he has since moved on, David will always have a place in his heart for the City of Kings. So beyond this intro, "I" refers to Colin.

Colin and David bring complementary areas of expertise to this guide to give you the low-down on the best places as well as the off-the-beaten-path spots.

The second edition of this guide has reduced the amount of space we devote to some subjects by including links for more information on the Lima City of Kings website. We are not trying to drive traffic, just trying to save space. For example, step-by-step instructions for the three walking tours occupied 20 pages of text, which grew to 30 with the bike tour. Instead of obliging uninterested readers to skip dozens of pages, those who are interested can find more details on the website.

In the second edition we have ventured into potentially controversial subjects such as bullfighting and "pepera" gangs. The purpose of the guide is to be useful for foreign visitors to Lima. So we beg your pardon if you're offended by anything, and ask you to use whichever information you find helpful and leave the rest.

Thanks for buying the book, and enjoy!

TABLE OF CONTENTS

History of Lima   1

Weather   8

Festivals and Events   11

Legal and Practical Matters   16

Health and Safety   20

Transportation   26

Neighborhoods   32

Where to Stay   38

Five Best Museums   44

Ten Things to Do in Lima   48

Restaurants   65

Nightlife   75

Parks and Plazas   81

Family-Friendly Lima   87

Lima Pueblos   90

Beyond Lima   93

About the Authors   99

Chapter 1
History of Lima

If I could go back in time to give myself one piece of advice before taking my first job in Latin America, I would tell myself to learn the history of my destination. You may not choose to read entire books on the subject, but understanding any place's trajectory will enhance your experience. Few cities in the Americas are as storied as the region of Lima, a cradle of civilization in the Americas.

PRE-COLUMBIAN LIMA

The Sacred City of Caral-Supe is located in the Lima department (Peru's equivalent to a "state"), 100 miles north of the city. At over 5,000 years old, Caral-Supe was home to the Americas' oldest known civilization.

Lima was continually home to thriving civilizations of fishermen who exploited the abundant marine resources of the sea. The population grew significantly after the Lima culture built irrigation canals which brought water from the Chillon, Rimac and Lurin rivers to what is now the heart of the city.

For most of the area's pre-Columbian history, the fishing and farming civilizations of Lima lived under the rule of cultures headquartered afar, such as the Chimu, Chavin, Wari and Inca cultures. The cultures which originated in and around Lima include the Caral, Lima (also known as Maranga), Chancay and Ichma.

Lima's ancient history can be seen not only in museums, but the "huacas" located throughout the city. Huacas are pre-Columbian ruins of holy sites, tombs and administrative centers. The most touristic are Pachacamac, Huaca Pucllana and Huaca Huallamarca. Pachacamac was the area's most important huaca, home to an oracle respected by succeeding conquerors including the Inca Culture.

There are dozens if not hundreds of huacas in Lima. The government does not have the resources to preserve all of them, or even protect them from squatters who seize the land to build informal housing. The sheer number of huacas illustrates how heavily populated Lima was before the colonial era.

The Incas subdued the inhabitants of Lima around 1450 A.D., less than 100 years before the arrival of a tiny band of Spaniards searching for a legendary city of gold.

CITY OF THE KINGS

Spanish conquistador Francisco Pizarro subdued the Inca Empire in 1533. But unlike Hernando Cortes after the conquest of the Aztecs in what is now Mexico City, Pizarro did not establish his colonial government on top of the Inca capital in Cusco. Instead, Pizarro founded "La Ciudad de los Reyes," or City of the Kings, in what is now Lima on January 18, 1535. Through mispronunciations in both Spanish and Quechua, the name morphed into "Lima."

Pizarro wanted a location on the sea to facilitate communication with Spain. The natural harbor in Callao could be converted into a high-traffic seaport. He also saw excellent defense positions in the San Lorenzo and El Fronton islands six miles from the coast.

Visitors to Lima today will see barren desert on the city's outskirts. But the Spaniards in 1535 found a green, fertile valley full of crops in what is now a concrete jungle. The thousands of inhabitants and historic ruins proved the area would support life.

Lima was designated as the crown's royal seat to rule the Spanish holdings on the continent, which included all of South America except Portuguese Brazil.

Just three years after the conquest, Manco Inca inspired a rebellion against the Spanish in 1536. Some 40,000 Inca soldiers led by Quizu Yupanqui surrounded Lima's 1,000 residents, which included 500 Spaniards. Spanish chronicles tell of the campfires visible on the Cerro San Cristobal mountain just north of the city center.

Competing versions of the story differ, but Pizarro's forces likely employed friendly tribes who resented Inca rule in a first line of defense while keeping Spanish forces and cavalry within the city in a strategy which prevailed over the Inca onslaught, ending Manco Inca's rebellion.

COLONIAL SEAT

Lima was destined to be an affluent city with a monopoly on South American trade, not to mention millions of Indian slaves. But the 1545 discovery of silver at Potosi in present-day Bolivia put Lima on a path of unimaginable wealth. Potosi is still the world's largest silver deposit ever discovered and Lima became a symbol of opulence, similar to tiny oil-rich countries of today like Qatar or Kuwait.

Under the religious monarchy of the Spanish crown, the Catholic Church was essentially an equal partner in government. The Lima diocese became the headquarters of the effort to convert millions of natives in South America to Christianity. Perusing Lima's cultural icons and history will inevitably lead you to churches, saints, processions and religious art because Catholicism played such an integral, if not founding, role in the city's development.

Saint Rose, the patron saint of Lima, became the first American-born to be canonized in 1671, and one of five saints in Peru. San Martin de Porres was the first black saint born in the Americas. Lima was the site of the Spanish Inquisition in South America, illustrated at an interesting museum next to Congress.

Spain had only recently expelled the Moors before colonizing the Americas, and Peru was largely settled by colonists from Spain's southern regions with the strongest Moorish footprint. Aside from the Moorish arches on colonial buildings, Lima's iconic wooden balconies are also a throwback to Arab architecture. The intricately designed screens allow women to observe the street without being seen. But the most visible cultural artifact Peru inherited from Spain's Moorish past was the "tapada limeña," a veil worn by the women of Lima which revealed only one eye. They would be called "burkas" today.

The kingdom of Spain changed hands in 1700 and the Bourbon Reforms spelled the start of a long decline in the wealth and power of Lima. The new monarchy established capitals in Bogota and Buenos Aires to rule more efficiently and reduced Peru's territory to a fraction of what it was.

RELUCTANT INDEPENDENCE

Creoles, or American-born Spaniards, were long frustrated with the monarchy's explicit preference for "peninsulares," or Spaniards born in Spain. But there was little appetite for independence in Peru, least of all in the capital. Lima was Spain's loyalist stronghold in South America.

The white Spaniards in Lima and greater Peru feared a revolution which would rearrange their position in the socioeconomic order. In 1780 Spanish forces put down an indigenous rebellion in Cusco led by Tupac Amaru II. Peru's elite would have been acutely aware of what would happen without the Spanish army if the millions of impoverished Indians in the Andean highlands ever united behind one leader.

While the millions of Indians posed one existential threat, the racial makeup of Lima before the 20th century looked more like Atlanta or Detroit than anywhere in Peru today. The Spaniards had imported so many African slaves that Afro-Peruvians were the city's largest ethnic demographic, about half of the population. A slave revolt was the greatest fear for Spanish colonists in Lima, especially after Haiti's 1791 revolution culminated in the massacre of every French colonist in the territory.

While there was no significant independence movement in Lima, a series of events around the world spelled change for Peru. The American Revolution inspired freedom fighters in Colombia and Argentina. The French Revolution spread democratic ideology across Europe, and the ensuing Napoleonic Wars weakened Spain to the point where its colonies effectively governed themselves.

During Spain's power vacuum, revolutionary leaders had declared independence for Gran Colombia and Argentina. Colombian and Argentine armies then battled to expel the Spanish from South America. The convergence of foreign armies in Peru would effectively impose independence from outside.

Revolutionary colonists favored independence while their reactionary counterparts saw the demise of the feudal system if it stayed under Spain, where a newly elected congress approved liberal reforms such as citizenship for the Indians and Africans.

Argentine general Jose de San Martin arrived in Peru virtually unopposed in 1820. He declared independence in Lima's Plaza de Armas on July 28, 1821, making Peru the last South American colony to be liberated from Spanish rule.

REPUBLICAN CAPITAL

Peru had no experience in democracy so, as seen across Latin America, the transition was messy. Dozens of presidents came and went, sometimes for only a few days, as regional strongmen known as "caudillos" led coups and factional wars.

In the mid-19th century, nutrient-rich manure from seabirds used as fertilizer in Europe ushered in an economic boom. The specific bird which creates this manure is native to the south Pacific, and its droppings had accumulated for millennia on Peru's Chincha Islands. The islands literally had mountains of this "guano," giving Peru a monopoly over the world's best fertilizer.

Peru's guano royalties in the 19th century are estimated to have exceeded oil revenues in today's Saudi Arabia or Norway. The windfall was mostly squandered by the elites, but the Guano Era helped build the institutions of the country.

In 1864 the guano wealth proved too much to resist for Spain, which had never recognized Peru's independence. The Spanish navy seized the islands in a brief war which saw Chile and other neighbors aid Peru in repelling their former colonial master. In the Battle of Callao on May 2, 1866, Peru's tiny navy aided by cannons at the Real Felipe Fortress fought Spain's attacking ships to a stalemate, ending the war.

President Ramon Castilla freed the slaves during the Guano Era. Without slave labor, Peru imported tens of thousands of Chinese "coolies" to build railroads which crisscrossed the interior. After serving the terms of their contracts, most of the Chinese immigrants relocated to Lima. In time they would leave an unmistakable footprint on the national culture.

Saltpeter nitrates replaced guano as Europe's fertilizer of choice in 1870, which quickly led to Peru's bankruptcy. The world's largest saltpeter deposit was in the Atacama Desert, which at the time spanned the territories of Bolivia, Chile and Peru. Control over saltpeter exports led to the War of the Pacific, which saw Peru allied with Bolivia against Chile.

After early victories in Bolivia and southern Peru, Chile defeated Peru's forces in battles at Chorrillos and Miraflores in 1881. Chilean soldiers sacked the city of Lima in what became a three-year occupation. The 1883 Treaty of Ancon ended the war and Peru ceded the Tarapaca province – home to valuable saltpeter deposits – and the port city of Arica to Chile.

The War of the Pacific and Chile's humiliating occupation of Lima left a wound on the Peruvian psyche. While government and business relations are friendly, Chile is Peru's historical nemesis and foreigners should be wise to the widespread anti-Chilean sentiment among Peruvians.

20TH CENTURY LIMA

Peru's recovery from bankruptcy and Chile's occupation began in the 1890s, when a third resource boom came with the mass commercialization of rubber. Peru and Brazil enjoyed a duopoly over naturally occurring rubber from the Para tree native to the Amazon rainforest. This economic cycle coincided with the rise of the "civilistas," the first civilian government of Peru which invested heavily in expanding the city.

The civilista leaders modeled Lima after Paris, with long avenues opening up on to public squares. The rubber boom ended in the early 1900s when a British engineer smuggled Para seeds out of Brazil and developed plantations on the tropical islands of Asia. But Peru enjoyed a second rubber boom in the 1940s when Japan blockaded Southeast Asia and Allied forces needed boots and tires for World War II.

The rubber boom attracted new immigrants to Lima, most notably from Italy and Japan. The Italian-Peruvian heritage is most evident in the boating culture of Callao's La Punta district, while the historic Japanese-Peruvian community is located in Jesus Maria. Like the Chinese, both cultures contributed to and enhanced Peru's cuisine.

Most of the city squares and avenues of Lima would have been developed between the 1890s and 1945. But the government's development plan would not keep up with the city's exploding population as farmers moved from rural areas to the cities for factory jobs, as seen around the world.

Lima was never a big city throughout most of Peru's trajectory, but rather a small enclave of elites. The cities of Cusco, Trujillo and Puno each had larger populations. But that was about to change due to the concentration of power and the emergence of an urban economy.

Peru's military overthrew the democratically elected government in 1968, ushering in 12 years of socialist policies. In true military fashion, General Juan Velasco Alvarado centralized decision making and the nation's institutions in the capital, which resulted in increased immigration to Lima from the countryside. Democracy was restored in 1980, but a rebellion by the Marxist guerrilla rebels, Shining Path, drove rural peasants caught in the crossfire to the capital, pushing the edges of metropolitan Lima far from the original city into desert shantytowns.

The population of Lima grew from 150,000 in 1812 to 224,000 in 1920, 828,000 in 1940, 2 million in 1961, 3.5 million in 1972, 4.7 million in 1987, 6.4 million in 1993 and 8.4 million in 2007. With a population of over 10 million today, Lima saw a whopping 4400% growth in less than a century.

An advancing economic crisis which started during the military dictatorship brought Peru to the brink of collapse in 1989. President Alberto Fujimori brought the economy back from the precipice in the 1990s, but in 2001 he resigned by fax from Japan. Disgraced by corruption of historic proportions (even on Peruvian standards), he is currently serving 25 years in prison for ordering extrajudicial killings.

LIMA TODAY

The disorderly growth of the 20th century has made Lima one of South America's most chaotic capitals. The main avenues are hopelessly insufficient, and few extend for more than a couple miles. Over half of the city's housing was built informally, or "extra-legally," by squatter settlements.

But as Peru emerged from the ruins of the 20th century, Lima is enjoying a renaissance reminiscent of its former glory. The city has attracted new investment in infrastructure and public transportation, which is improving commutes. Glistening apartment buildings make up much of the urban landscape as, for the first time in the city's history, the middle and upper classes comprise more than half of the population.

The waves of immigration changed Lima's ethnic identity from a mostly white-and-black city to a melting pot of every color of the rainbow. The mixing of European music with Afro-Peruvian rhythms and Andean sounds spawned new genres including criolla, cumbia and chicha.

Peruvian cuisine is one of Latin America's most varied, winning the distinction of world's best culinary destination for five consecutive years and making Lima the gastronomic capital of the continent.

The economic boom has also made Lima one of Latin America's safest big cities as Peru's poverty was cut by two thirds. Many cities in the United States have higher crime rates than Lima's.

Lima has seen some hard times, but there is a palpable optimism in the air as most residents see a bright future.

GOING FURTHER

To learn more about Lima and its role in greater Peru, below is a list of resources to help you go down the rabbit hole.

Books

Lima: A Cultural History – Latin American literature professor James Higgins dedicated his life to studying Peru and this text is the best out there on Lima's culture with no focus on tourism whatsoever.

The Other Path – Economist Hernando de Soto's research into Lima's informal economies inspired the World Bank's Ease of Doing Business rankings. This may be a little wonkish for anybody who isn't an economics nerd, but no other book captures the corruption and chaos that made Lima what it is today.

Conversation in the Cathedral – This book, arguably the best novel by Nobel laureate Mario Vargas Llosa, is set in 1950s Lima under the dictatorship of Manuel Odria. It captures cynicism, classism, racism and chaos in the soul of Lima.

A World For Julius – A biting critique of the insularity and pettiness of Lima's upper class, told from the perspective of a young boy in an elite family.

The Peru Reader – Duke University Press put together this collection of essays, speeches and passages from the most important books and news events across Peru's history. The best all-in-one source for Peruvian history in English.

Conquest of the Incas – Classic account told by John Hemming of the most important event in Peru's history: when the native Peruvians came under control of the Spanish. Another great account of the same story is Last Days of the Incas by Kim MacQuarrie.

Film

Milk of Sorrow – The only Peruvian film nominated for an Oscar follows a woman who was brought to the shantytown slums outside Lima to escape the violence of the armed conflict with the Shining Path. This is a great primer for those doing the Lima Shantytown Tour.

Asu Mare – Hilarious memoir based on the life of Peruvian comedian Carlos Alcantara. You may have to search to find this one subtitled, but it is the only comedy on this list.

Magallanes – Years after the armed conflict ended, a former soldier in Lima recognizes a peasant woman he knew was victimized by army officers. His attempts to reconcile the human-rights abuses of the past lead to violence.

No Se Lo Digas a Nadie – Now a television commentator and opinion journalist, Jaime Bayly rose to prominence for this coming-out tale of growing up gay in upper-class Lima.

Caido del Cielo (Fallen from Heaven) – This may not be available in subtitles. But if you can find it, this classic is the most acclaimed film depicting 1950s Lima. Shot in the 1980s by Peru's preeminent director, Francisco Lombardi, the film is based on a book by award-winning author Julio Ramon Ribeyro.

Web

Peru has three English-language news sites in Peru Reports, Peruvian Times and Living in Peru. LimaCityKings.com is our city guide and culture blog to complement this book.

The national letter of record is the center-right El Comercio, whose main competition is the center-left La Republica. Gestion's salmon-pink color ala Financial Times signals its focus on business and economics. The leading news magazine is Caretas.

En Lima offers the best event calendar on the web. Lima Gris is the top alternative culture rag, akin to the bimonthly freebies in many American cities. Lima la Unica is an interesting aggregator of Lima culture and history through photos, videos and articles on Facebook.

The city's official cultural website is Lima Cultura. But the best place to find official city event info is the Municipality of Lima Facebook page.

Chapter 2
Weather

Despite being located in the tropics, Lima is surprisingly mild. Temperatures stay within 60 and 85 degrees Fahrenheit (15 and 30 degrees Celsius). Lima's climate comes courtesy of the Humboldt Current, cold water which sweeps up from Antarctica and cools the Pacific Coast of lower South America. While temperatures are mild, Lima's humidity will be the greatest challenge for those planning a long stay.

WHAT TO WEAR

Lima is comfortable throughout the year, but it does get cold in the winter and some visitors may prefer air conditioning in the summer.

Because Lima is located in the Southern Hemisphere, the seasons are inverted from North America and Europe. The warmest months, when sweaty afternoon temperatures rise to the mid 80s, are January through March. The cold and cloudy months of July through September cool down to the low 60s.

While highs of around 85 degrees in January and February may not seem too bad, the humidity brings the heat index into difficult territory. T-shirts and shorts are the norm. In February and March, socks can be too much, so bring sandals.

For winter from July through September, a hooded sweatshirt or light jacket are needed for the cold days and nights. You may see Peruvians wearing thick winter coats or ski caps in the winter, but these are probably migrants from the sweltering regions of the north or the Amazon jungle. If you're not from southern Florida or Louisiana, you will be fine in a normal jacket.

The in-between months of April, May and June are the fall season, while October, November and December form the South American spring. These months generally see a mix of overcast and sunny skies with moderate temperatures in the low 70s during the day and high 60s at night.

The Sun: a Dangerous Friend

Fair-skinned people should wear sunblock whenever they will be outside for more than an hour, even in the winter months when the cold and clouds can be deceptive. I am fair-skinned and I was burned red "as a shrimp" – as they say in Peru – during a Mistura food festival where the pictures clearly show an overcast sky. Remember that Lima is a tropical region and the strength of the sun overpowers the thickest winter clouds.

Humidity

Lima is the world's second largest city located in a desert (after Cairo, Egypt). The good news is that it never rains, or at least it doesn't yield what we in the American Midwest would consider rain with 0.3 inches of precipitation per year. Occasionally in the winter there are wet particles slowly descending from the sky. Known as "garua," it is more than a mist but less than a drizzle. You will never need an umbrella.

The Humboldt Current's cold waters don't evaporate enough to produce rain, but it does create the dense, gray fog that blankets the city from June through October. If you come during those months, you may not glimpse the sun at all. This ever-present fog that engulfs the city, called "neblina" by Limeños, has inspired one of Lima's nicknames, "La Gris" (The Gray One).

So with virtually no rain, or maybe because of it, Lima is unbelievably humid. To illustrate how humid it is, imagine you have just washed your clothes. If you hang them up inside the house, they will never dry. They will stay wet forever and mold. Wet clothes must be hung up outside under the sun, even in winter.

Even under the tropical sun, the clothes won't get completely dry. Using a clothes dryer is one way to dry your clothes completely, but few homes have dryers. You can take your clothes to a local Laundromat which will have dryers, but that can be expensive and time-consuming.

We use a clothes iron with no water in it to dry clothes after they have hung in the sun for a day. The heat from the iron evaporates the remaining moisture in the clothes.

Storing clothes, books or sports equipment in closets or boxes can put your things at risk of mold. In one of his memoirs, Mario Vargas Llosa lived in Paris for several years. When he returned to his family home in Lima, he found his prized book collection in the attic had completely rotted. The books had to be thrown away.

Sunlight can help kill mold and other fungi, so it's important to open up closets and drawers every day for people who will be here long-term. Remove suits and clothes which are rarely worn from the closet to hang in the sun once every month or two. Then they return to the closet inside zipped-up garment bags.

Perfect Climate

This humid desert may be the world's strangest climate, and it has driven more than a few foreigners out of their wits. But while Lima may not be the ideal weather for everybody, the chroniclers of the colonial era gushed over it. They believed for hundreds of years that they had found the world's perfect climate.

Some expats in Peru point to the founding date in January and conclude that Pizarro made a mistake in selecting the location because it would have been warm and sunny, as opposed to cold and dreary if he had landed in July or August.

I doubt he would have cared. In a time when cities were wiped out by famine or disease, people of the 16th century did not have the same priorities. Hundreds of years before the Industrial Revolution and without the comforts of modern technology, their main priority was whether a region could support life. And the thousands of natives living in a fertile, green valley provided all the proof they needed. The millennial ruins were the icing on the cake.

You can always see the bright side of Lima's climate and remember that it never rains. The humidity and winter fog are a small price to pay. Plus, the Humboldt Current is responsible for Peru's waters being home to some of the world's largest fish populations. Without the cold water, the gastronomy of Lima may not have become what it is today – the best food in Latin America!

Chapter 3
Festivals and Events

If you have the luxury to plan your trip to Lima whenever you like, the biggest festivals and events in the city are listed below. We recommend Mistura, the largest food festival in Latin America.

BEACH SEASON

The Humboldt Current blankets Lima in cloudy dreariness for at least six months per year. But from January through March, the sun emerges and the people of Lima hit the beach.

For more info on Lima's beaches, see Chapter 16. But suffice to say the only time to bask in the sun is the South American summer from January through March.

ANNIVERSARY OF LIMA

On January 18, 1535, Pizarro founded the capital as La Ciudad de los Reyes (City of Kings). But the new colonists and indigenous Peruvians came to call the new capital "Lima," a product of joint mispronunciations in Quechua and Spanish. "City of Kings" was relegated to a nickname.

Today, the city of Lima holds small celebrations downtown featuring live music, fireworks, traditional dances, the Peruvian Paso horses and plenty of eating and drinking.

PERUVIAN PASO HORSE COMPETITION

The Peruvian Paso breed descended from Arabian horses is showcased at competitions by leading breeders from across Peru. The Peruvian Paso is a special breed whose compact muscles make high vertical and wide horizontal strides to ensure a smooth ride.

As in most of the world, equestrian culture is reserved for people with money. The shows feature top-quality Creole cuisine on large haciendas with nice views, where Peru's elite drink Johnny Walker black wearing a sombrero, white dress shirt and either khakis or jeans with boots.

There are festivals and competitions throughout the year, but the most important contests are the Traditional Summer Contest in February, the Official National Contest in April and the Amancaes contest in July. Each of these shows is held in the Lurin district just south of the city.

A smaller contest is held in September just east of the city in Cieneguilla, and others are held in January and December in Cañete and Huaral, small towns located within Lima department but a day trip from the city.

You can find an official schedule of competitions throughout Peru at the National Association of Peruvian Paso Horse Breeders and Owners (ANCPCPP) official website: ancpcpp.org.pe.

To see the Peruvian Paso horses anytime, you can visit traditional family ranches such as Hacienda Mamacona, where two of the largest competitions are held, or Hacienda Los Ficus.

WINE AND PISCO FESTIVAL

The Festival de la Vendimia is a wine festival in Lima's old grape-producing district of Surco. The annual fair features plenty of grape-based alcohol in wine and pisco, Peru's national spirit, as well as cuisine, live music and the traditional Afro-Peruvian dance, "festejo."

While Surco does not have the vineyards of a century ago, the wine and pisco tradition continues in Surco's Plaza de Armas every year. The festival is known for its beauty pageant, in which barefoot contestants dressed in short skirts step on grapes to extract the juice.

While the festival is dedicated to alcohol, it is fairly family-friendly during the daytime. The beauty pageant around 5 p.m. is when it becomes more adult-oriented, the focus on alcohol surpasses food, an amphitheater hosts live music and the crowds get too thick to take care of small children.

The timing of the Vendimia Festival has changed over the years, but the Surco district has seemed to have recently settled on May.

FIESTAS PATRIAS

On July 28, 1821, Argentine liberator Jose de San Martin declared independence for Peru in Lima's main square. Today, "Fiestas Patrias" mark a full week of festivals and parties celebrating independence. It is effectively a weeklong holiday.

Many Lima residents choose to escape the city during Fiestas Patrias to visit cities and towns around the country. For those who stay, there are daily festivities downtown and in every neighborhood throughout the city.

Each district will hold a small fair in their main park or plaza – usually near the municipal building – featuring gastronomy, pisco and cocktails, live music and dancing.

The Plaza de Armas, Parque de la Reserva and Parque de Las Leyendas host the largest celebrations with fireworks and all the other bells and whistles. For info on dates and times, see the Lima city government's Facebook page (facebook.com/MuniLima) in the weeks leading up to the event.

On July 28, the Plaza de Armas is a center of action when the president attends an annual mass at the Cathedral of Lima led by the Lima archbishop which concludes in singing the Te Deum hymn. The president then delivers a legally mandated Message to the Nation speech before Congress.

The main Fiestas Patrias event in Lima is the Great Military Parade on July 29, when Peru's military shows off all its guns, bazookas, tanks, uniforms ranging from jungle warfare to urban riots, cavalry and all other rank of soldier in a daylong march down Brasil Avenue.

The Te Deum hymn, Message to the Nation and Great Military Parade are each broadcast across all of Peru's national television channels.

MISTURA FOOD FESTIVAL

Mistura is the largest food festival in Latin America and, at the time of this publication, Peru holds five consecutive World Travel Awards for Best Culinary Destination.

The festival showcases traditional dishes from all of Peru's regions and world-renowned chefs. In addition to food, there is live music and entertainment. The week-long festival is held in mid-September. See the website for more details: mistura.pe.

If there is one event we recommend above all others, especially for foodies, it is Mistura. Here are some tips:

Go on a weekday to avoid the crowds.

Buy anything the celebrity chefs make.

Don't buy food tickets at the entrance. Food is purchased with tickets, not cash. So the first ticket stand after the entrance has long lines while most other ticket stands are empty.

Skip the stuff you can get anytime. If you are going to be in Lima for more than a week or so, you don't need to get a pork sandwich from El Chinito at Mistura, as good as they are. Get something from another region or something you won't see again.

Always ask for the half order. You have only so much space in the stomach, and so many things to try.

Blow some cash. I buy at least 300 soles ($90) of tickets.

SEÑOR DE LOS MILAGROS

The Lord of Miracles celebrations are South America's largest Catholic processions. Pictured at the beginning of this chapter, the image is paraded around downtown Lima on October 18, 19 and 28 as well as one other date which has recently been October 1 but is subject to change. Downtown Lima is normally quite safe before 9 p.m., but is even more so during Señor de los Milagros. Even if you're not religious, you can appreciate the tradition's strong roots in this deeply Catholic city.

When Peru was a Spanish colony in 1651, an Angolan slave painted the image of Jesus Christ on the wall of a slave quarters on the site of what is now La Iglesia de las Nazarenas on Tacna Avenue in downtown Lima.

In 1655 an earthquake damaged much of the city but left the image intact. In 1687 the image survived another earthquake, prompting a prominent Spaniard to hold the first Señor de los Milagros procession, parading a replica of the image around the city.

What began as an Afro-Peruvian tradition was increasingly adopted by Lima's Creole middle classes in the 18th century. In 1746 an 8.6-magnitude earthquake destroyed Lima, killing as many as 11,000 people in a city of just 60,000.

The image survived this earthquake as well and today the Señor de los Milagros Brotherhood, one of the most esteemed orders in the Lima archdiocese, carries a one-ton effigy in its annual processions.

The replica image is paraded on various routes on different days to the churches of downtown Lima, Barrios Altos, Breña and La Victoria. Hundreds of thousands flock to the city center to attend Mass, glimpse the procession, say a prayer or light a candle at the original image.

October is known as the "purple month" in Lima, and everybody at the processions wears something purple as a symbol of penitence. It is also customary to eat the event's signature snack, the Turron de Doña Pepa.

The effigy moves so slow that there is no rush to see it. The routes are covered during a whole day. While it is not easy to approach the replica image, there are enough people coming and going at any given time that staying with the crowd and patiently advancing forward as others leave will allow you to get pretty close.

The original image at Church of the Nazarenes is easily visited, and a stall sells candles and other offerings.

For specific dates and routes, see the Archdiocese of Lima website at arzobispadodelima.org. For a more detailed description with pictures and videos, visit goo.gl/bMVy9b.

BULLFIGHTING

Plaza de Acho in Rimac, the oldest bullring in the Americas, hosts the annual bullfighting season known as Feria del Señor de los Milagros. The short season sees "corridas" on six Sundays from late October to early December. Tickets range from $100 to $600.

Like horse competitions, bullfighting is very much an upper-class interest in Lima and throughout Latin America. Contrary to what I thought, bullfighting is not an all-men's affair. There are plenty of upper-class women cheering on their favorite men in tights which accentuate their masculinity.

Bullfighting is, as expected, a drinking affair. Beers inside the plaza cost 15 soles ($5). They also sell chilcanos (pisco and ginger ale) and other cocktails. Aficionados bring boots filled with sangria, wine or their liquor of choice.

The Plaza de Acho is an easy walk from downtown Lima. Walk north on Abancay Avenue until you cross the Rimac River. Follow the crowds after the bridge straight through the intersection.

You can buy padded seats, sombreros, beer and an inexpensive meal outside the plaza. Everything is more expensive inside. Purchase tickets at TuEntrada.com.pe or their booths inside Vivanco and Plaza Vea supermarkets.

Be warned. The bulls are killed in what many deem a bloody, cruel and inhumane diversion which should be banned around the world.

To learn more about bullfighting in Lima, visit goo.gl/NemtWA.

Chapter 4
Legal and Practical Matters

TOURIST VISAS

Citizens from the United States, Canada, EU countries, Switzerland and Australia receive a tourist visa on arrival. Peru's immigration office sets the maximum amount of time as a tourist in Peru at 183 days per calendar year. Anything beyond 183 days requires a resident visa.

Requirements

Entry requirements include a passport and proof of onward travel. While immigration officials have never asked me for proof of onward travel despite entering Peru dozens of times with no onward travel planned before I got a resident visa, your airline may legally request it before they allow you to board your flight.

Peru does not require any vaccinations, but the health ministry recommends the yellow-fever vaccine for those looking to visit jungle regions of Amazonas, Loreto, San Martin, Ucayali, Junin or Madre de Dios.

Penalty for Overstaying

If you overstay your visa, you will be required to pay $1 for each day you overstayed. For example, if you arrived in Peru on January 1 and remained in the country until December 31, you'd be required to pay $275 upon departure.

Due to the potential for change regarding these rules, which is common, we recommend confirming this information with the government site for your home country or with a Peruvian embassy.

MONEY

The local currency is the Peruvian Sol (PEN), or "sol" for short. The plural pronunciation, "soles," is two syllables (SO-lays). The exchange rate used in this guide is $0.30 = S/ 1, or $1 = S/ 3.38, with generous rounding to even numbers. But that rate will likely change by the time you read this book.

ATMs

Peru's ATMs accept most international debit and credit cards, though the maximum withdrawal can vary. In my experience, the Spanish banks' (BBVA Continental, Santander) limits are on the lower end of the spectrum at around 400 soles ($140). Scotiabank is on the higher end with limits of 1,000 soles ($360). And the Peruvian banks (BCP, Interbank) are a happy medium with limits around 700 soles ($250).

If withdrawing a large amount, ATMs will probably give you 100-sol bills and maybe even a 200-sol note. These are difficult or impossible to change in neighborhood shops and taxis. In Peru, the burden is on the customer to have correct change or small bills.

If you do change a 100-sol or 200-sol note, do so in a business you trust. Peru leads the world in counterfeiting, and unscrupulous taxi drivers and shop owners specifically look for tourists to pass counterfeits.

Cash vs. Plastic

Cash is king in Peru. Credit is only accepted by a few retailers. Taxi drivers hailed in the street only take cash. A good way to guess if a business takes credit is if it's a corporate chain. A Peruvian corporate chain or international chain will accept any card with the Visa or MasterCard logo. If it's not a corporate chain, a nice restaurant or high-end bar, assume that it will only accept cash.

Safety Tip: Don't walk around with debit and credit cards if you don't need them. In the event of a robbery, you'll minimize the risk of losing one or more of your cards and having to suspend accounts and get replacement cards. Also, some forced robberies known as "express kidnappings" involve taking victims in taxis to a string of ATMs to max out the daily withdrawal limit.

Tipping

Tipping is not expected at cheap restaurants. Servers at the nicer restaurants expect 10 percent. If the service was good or you intend to come back, leave a tip.

Tipping bartenders and wait staff in bars and clubs is not expected, but if you want to become a regular at a certain venue, set a friendly tone from the start. If you're in the VIP section of a club, definitely tip the person who took care of you for the night.

SAMPLE COSTS

Accommodations in Lima range from cheap beds in hostel dorms to five-star hotels. In the middle, there's a wide range of budget hotel options, plus short-term room and apartment rentals.

- Hostel dorm beds: 20 soles ($6) and up.
- Budget hotel rooms: 80 soles ($25) and up.

Peruvian food can be a bargain at limited-menu restaurants, called "menus." These eateries package a soup or appetizer with a small lunch and juice for as little as 7 soles ($2).

- Bottle of water: 2 soles ($0.60)
- Typical set lunch with juice at a menu: 7 to 15 soles ($2 to $4.50)
- Dinner (not including drinks) at a restaurant in Parque Kennedy: 30 to 50 soles ($9 to $15)

Prices of beers and cocktails can vary depending on the district.

- 21-ounce domestic beer from a store: 5 soles ($1.50)
- Domestic beer at a bar or club (12 ounces): 10 soles ($3)
- Pisco sours, mojitos and other cocktails: 20+ soles ($6+)

Transportation costs:

- Bus: 0.50 to 1.50 soles
- Taxi: 5 to 30 soles ($2 to $9)
- Metropolitano (rapid-bus system): 2.50 soles
- Metro (light-rail train): 1.50 soles

The cost of travel and living in Peru used to be lower than in Brazil, Argentina, Chile and Uruguay, but its red-hot economy is changing that. Budgets will vary widely based on style of travel and the amount of partying one does.

- Minimum Daily Tourism Budget: $35
- Minimum Monthly Budget: $1,000

STAYING CONNECTED

Voltage Requirements

Electricity in Peru is 220 volts and 60 cycles AC. Peru's electric outlets are designed to accept both kinds of two-pronged plugs: those with flat blades common in the U.S. and those with round pins used in Europe.

To avoid any potential damage, double-check that your chargers or electrical devices are compatible with 220 volts. If your devices are not compatible, you'll have to use a converter. These are cheap and easy to find on arrival.

NOTE: I shave my head with professional hair clippers, and I have absentmindedly burned out two American clippers in Peru because I forgot to use the converter. So be mindful of voltage!

Internet and Wi-Fi

Internet access is easy to come by in Lima. Most visitors will be able to access the internet via Wi-Fi in their hotels, hostels or apartment rentals. An increasing number of parks and restaurants offer free access, such as Parque Kennedy in Miraflores.

Another option is to use the local internet cafes. You'll find them everywhere – not only in Lima but throughout Peru – offering cheap internet access and printing services.

Internet speeds aren't as fast as your average connections in Western cities, but they're sufficient for email, Facebook, uploading photos and Skype.

Local Cell Phone Services

The cell phone carriers in Peru are Claro, Movistar, Entel, Bitel and Virgin Mobile.

A new crime-fighting law requires Peruvian identification to obtain a SIM card, so tourists are no longer allowed to have local phone numbers. Because the law and telecommunications products are constantly changing, visit a storefront from any of the companies above to inquire further.

Chapter 5
Health and Safety

Disclaimer. This does not constitute professional medical advice, nor do the authors bear any responsibility for services provided by the entities below.

Tap Water

Do not drink the tap water in Lima or anywhere in Peru. Drink bottled water or tap water which has been boiled.

Humidity

The humidity can be difficult for people with respiratory issues. If you find yourself wheezing or coughing in the winter months, an inhaler can alleviate the symptoms. Salbutamol is sold over the counter for about 10 soles ($3). If you have asthma or other serious bronchial problems, Lima may not be a viable place to live long term.

Another challenge the humidity poses is what Peruvians call "hongos," which means "fungus" or "mushrooms." But what they're referring to in Lima is what we in the United States call "Athlete's Foot," common among teenage athletes who drench their socks playing sports and the skin of their feet become breeding grounds for these itchy fungi.

Lima is so humid, however, you don't have to be an athlete to get it anywhere on your body. Make sure you completely dry yourself after bathing to avoid breeding grounds. Anti-fungal creams are sold at all pharmacies.

Immunizations and Malaria

The Hepatitis B vaccine is recommended for travelers who plan to be in contact with local populations for an extended time, especially in the departments of Amazonas, Loreto, San Martin, Ucayali, Junin and Madre de Dios. The yellow fever vaccine is recommended for travelers to areas in those departments below 7,546ft (2,300m) in elevation.

Malaria is not an issue for visitors to Lima, Cusco and Machu Picchu. If your itinerary includes the Amazon rainforest, visit the CDC website's map of Peru's areas where malaria is a risk.

HOSPITALS AND CLINICS

Medical care in Lima is generally good, especially at the private clinics, where you'll often find Western-trained, English-speaking doctors. Even at these upscale clinics, services are likely to be less expensive than you'd find in the United States or Europe.

Don't let the term "clinic" mislead you. Many of Lima's largest private clinics feature emergency rooms and are open 24 hours a day.

Regardless of whether you are seeking services as a tourist passing through town or as a resident in Lima, patients are often required to pay for medical services in advance. For example, if your specialist orders X-rays, you'll likely have to pay for the X-rays before they can be taken.

Below is a short list of hospitals in Lima's upscale neighborhoods.

Clinica Anglo Americana
Cl. Alfredo Salazar 350, San Isidro
Tel: (1) 616-8900
www.angloamericana.com.pe

Offering a range of specialists and services, the modern Clinica Anglo Americana is one of the higher-end private clinics in Lima. This is where Dave chose to go when seeking an English-speaking orthopedist to treat his lower back pain. He was seen by Dr. Carlos Vildozola, who had spent 20 years working in New York and Connecticut before returning to Peru. It is the hospital of choice among the embassy circuit and corporate expat community.

Clinica El Golf
Av. Aurelio Miro Quesada 1030, San Isidro
Tel: (1) 613-0000
www.sanna.pe/clinicas/el-golf-lima

A private clinic located in one of the most upscale neighborhoods in Lima and named after the elite country club in San Isidro. Opened in 1996, Clinica El Golf features 155 doctors in over 30 fields, and is one clinic in the SANNA hospital network, a partner of John Hopkins School of Medicine with locations in La

Molina, San Borja and other cities in Peru.

Clinica Good Hope
Malecon Balta 956, Miraflores
Tel: (1) 610-7300
www.goodhope.org.pe

Clinica Good Hope is a private clinic located conveniently in Miraflores. Dave went here twice within his first few weeks in Lima, once for stomach discomfort after drinking tap water and the second due to an allergic reaction.

Clinica San Felipe
Av. Gregorio Escobedo 650, Jesus Maria
Tel: (1) 219-5000
www.clinicasanfelipe.com

The six-floor Clinica San Felipe is a little further from Miraflores than some of the other clinics mentioned here, but it's another recommended option for international tourists. In 2012 the clinic underwent major renovations, tripling its capacity.

Clinica San Pablo
Av. El Polo 789, Surco
Tel: (1) 610-3333
www.sanpablo.com.pe

Clinica San Pablo offers multiple locations throughout Lima, as well as across Peru. It's another private clinic with a good reputation.

Hospital Santa Rosa
Av. Bolivar Cuadra 8, Pueblo Libre
Tel: (1) 615-8200
www.hsr.gob.pe

Hospital Santa Rosa in Pueblo Libre is a public hospital for Peruvians with no health insurance. Colin paid 36 soles ($11) for seven stitches with anesthesia in 2013. His wife underwent an appendectomy while pregnant, which cost 980 soles ($320) including two nights' stay.

This is obviously not an upscale hospital. The disadvantages to such accessible healthcare are the crowds and long waits. The campus is packed, and you can wait hours for attention. But if you can't afford the other clinics, keep Santa Rosa in mind.

EsSalud
Various locations

EsSalud is Peru's state healthcare network. All Peruvian citizens and legal residents who are formally employed are insured under the EsSalud program. But given only one in four workers is formally employed, it's hardly the National Health Service of the United Kingdom.

Do not go to an EsSalud hospital. If you're going to go public, you might as well go to an inexpensive facility like Santa Rosa. And if you're going to pay EsSalud prices, you might as well go to a private hospital like the others listed here.

For additional suggestions, see the U.S. embassy website's Medical Assistance page for a list of recommended doctors.

Pharmacies

Many of the drugs you're required to have a prescription for in Western countries are available over the counter in Peru. This is not a license to get whatever you want, but it does make it easier to refill maintenance medications.

We recommend sticking to the major pharmacy chains like Mifarma and Inkafarma. Pirated medications, which are at best ineffective and at worst contaminated, are common in the independent drugstores of downtown Lima and poor districts.

CRIME AND DANGERS

Earthquakes

Peru is an earthquake-prone country due to its location between the Nazca and South American Plates. Most of these quakes are minor, registering 4 or 5 on the Richter scale. They're enough to be felt, but not strong enough to cause structural damage. Lima's modern buildings have been constructed to withstand these small to moderate earthquakes.

However, experts predict that at least 10,000 people would die if a large-scale earthquake were to hit Lima. Nearly all of the casualties would come from informal housing in Lima's poorer districts built on the hillsides of mountains.

La Molina is the only upscale district facing significant risk in the event of an earthquake. The suburb-like area on the eastern edge of the city was developed on loose soil.

There are many myths and misconceptions about how to stay safe during an earthquake. Visit earthquakecountry.org for the best information.

Thieves

The security situation in the tourist parts of Lima is quite good, and crime in Peru is significantly lower than in most of Latin America. Common street crime is the biggest concern. There are things you can do to mitigate risk. Use good judgment and you should be fine. When in doubt, trust your instincts.

Pickpockets operate in crowded areas such as downtown Lima, buses, parades, street markets and concerts.

To be safe, take only what you need with you. If you must take a debit or credit

e and leave the rest locked up at your accommodation. Take only
l for the day. Keep your wallet, money, cell phone and any
ur front pockets.

t flash your smartphone in public. If you need to consult this guide, maps
or anything else, be conscious of who is around you.

Be careful where you place your handbags or backpacks in cafes and
restaurants. Thieves can easily walk off with a purse slung over a chair without the
owner knowing. Also pay close attention to your belongings when using buses.

In hostels and hotels, take advantage of lockers and safes.

Traffic Light Robberies

Some gangs take advantage of congested roads and rob passengers in vehicles
stopped in traffic. If your window is down, they may simply grab your jewelry,
smartphone, camera or bag. Many of these thieves work from motorcycles, where
they can escape unimpeded by traffic. The U.S. Department of State website warns
they may even break your window, so some Peruvians recommend you leave it
slightly open, or "cracked," to make it harder to break.

Taxis

The taxi industry used to be notorious for drivers who work with criminal
gangs to rob unsuspecting passengers. But the city of Lima has made great strides
in registering taxi drivers, driving down the risk of taxi assaults to foreigners visiting
Lima and greater Peru.

The safest way to use taxis in Lima is by using a telephone-dispatch service or
web app such as Uber, Easy Taxi or Taxibeat. If you're staying at a hotel, hostel or
apartment building with a security desk, they can call a taxi for you.

While hailing taxis from the street is more practical, you must learn the rules.
You don't simply hail a taxi and tell the driver where you're going. If you do this, at
the very least you will be overcharged.

Safe taxis are registered with the city's official ministry of urban transport,
SETAME. Registered taxi drivers will have the SETAME sticker prominently
displayed on the windshield.

Another safety indicator to look for is a company logo or yellow-and-black
checkerboard painted on the door, or the license plate painted on the body of the
car.

Get a feel for the driver. If he seems suspicious, let him go.

Once you have hailed a taxi, determine the price beforehand because Peruvian
taxis don't have meters. The price is negotiated based on the destination. Tell the
taxi where you're going and he'll quote you a price. You can accept, decline or
negotiate.

Only get in the cab once you've determined the safety of the driver and agreed
upon a price.

Peperas

The term, "pepera," refers to gangs who drug unsuspecting victims in bars and
nightclubs in order to incapacitate and rob them later. They put crushed pills –

usually clonazepam – into their victims' drinks.

The pepera gangs use attractive women to get close to male targets and slip drugs into their drinks. In most cases, the unsuspecting victims never see the men working with these women behind the scenes.

Like men, women should never accept a drink if they didn't see it prepared. The same drugs used to rob men are also used in sexual assaults against unsuspecting women. Going out in groups and promising not to separate is a good way to mitigate the risk of being drugged, which can result in overdose.

Unfortunately the pepera risk isn't confined to one area or even socioeconomic level. Pepera gangs operate throughout the city and greater Peru. The safest places to avoid them, however, would be upscale bars catering to older crowds which don't have blaring music or patrons getting drunk.

"Brichera" is slang for a Peruvian woman who aims to meet foreign men, specifically from Western countries in North America or Europe. Likewise, Peruvian men aiming to meet Western women are known as "bricheros."

"Brichera" implies that the woman is seeking to benefit financially by legally immigrating to a rich country or otherwise climb the social ladder via relationships with foreign men. The term is based on the English term, "bridge," because they were jokingly seen as bridging the culture gap between Peru and the West. While many of these men and women may simply be attracted to foreigners, it is an insulting term in Peru.

Men should be wary of women who are suspiciously forward or even aggressive. Whether she's a brichera or a pepera, she probably has ulterior motives. Both kinds are common anywhere tourists are known to congregate, especially Parque Kennedy and Calle de las Pizzas in Miraflores.

Chapter 6
Transportation

Lima is located midway down Peru's Pacific Coast. The convenient location between North America and most destinations in South America have made the Lima airport the top hub on the continent. But the Andes Mountains flanking the city on the east which run up and down Peru make road transportation time-consuming and sometimes dangerous.

GETTING THERE AND AWAY

By Plane

Lima's Jorge Chavez International Airport (LIM) is located in Callao, a 30-minute taxi ride from Miraflores. Lima is served by international, regional and domestic carriers. American, Delta, JetBlue, LAN, Avianca, Spirit and United are a few of the companies serving Lima from the United States alone. Just before publishing this guide's second edition, the Ryanair founders announced the launch of Viva Air Peru to offer domestic flights for as little as $20.

To safely travel from the airport to your accommodation upon arrival, book a safe taxi at the row of kiosks just after exiting customs with your baggage. Prices from these official taxis are always changing, but at the time of this edition a ride to Miraflores should cost 50 soles ($15).

Be conscious of how much space you need. If you have more than two passengers with two suitcases each, you probably won't fit in a standard Peruvian taxi. Look for CMV Taxi, whose desk is on the right end of this row of kiosks. They offer Honda Pilot SUVs for families and small groups.

By Bus

Lima is located along the Pan-American Highway, which runs between Alaska and the southern tip of Argentina. This is the main route for all road traffic moving up or down the coast of Peru.

Buses run between Lima and all of Peru's major cities and most of the smaller cities as well. If you are going to a very remote, small town, you may need to take a bus from Lima to the local provincial capital before changing buses to your pueblo.

You can also book buses to international cities including La Paz, Quito and Cali – all journeys of more than 24 hours which probably aren't worth the hassle unless you really need to save a few bucks.

Lima has a centralized bus terminal, Gran Terminal Terrestre, but its location at the Plaza Norte shopping mall in Independencia is inconvenient for where most international visitors and residents will stay.

The standard option for foreigners to take a bus is to select a company which operates out of an independent terminal. The most comfortable and slightly pricier options include Cruz del Sur in Surco and Oltursa in San Isidro.

Hermanos Flores is my choice because it is located in a district of several bus companies downtown at the intersection of 28 de Julio Avenue and the Via Expresa, or on the other side of the highway from Parque de la Exposicion. In case Hermanos Flores is sold out for the destination I want, there are plenty of other companies next door.

Warning: Do not nickel-and-dime your regional bus trip. Traffic fatalities involving provincial buses, especially in the rural highlands, are common in Peru. Accidents in which dozens perish regularly make national news, and they are almost always small companies with dirt-cheap fares. Choose a major company at the more expensive end of the spectrum which has a website, or one of the companies mentioned here.

GETTING AROUND THE CITY

Lima's streets are mostly laid out in a grid, but ending avenues, roundabouts and other inconsistencies disrupt the organization. In fact, "organization" is almost a misnomer given the chaotic expansion of Lima in the 20th century. The sustained explosions in population have created a sprawling city with insufficient avenues, highways and public transportation.

The result is aggressive drivers who don't necessarily slow down for pedestrians or cyclists. The residential streets of central districts aren't safe either as speeding commuters look to beat the impossible traffic of the avenues.

Planning a trip across the city can be confusing since few avenues go very far. It's more likely that you'll have to make a series of turns and detours on side streets, and most taxi rides will inevitably take you on bizarre routes as well.

By Taxi

Lima's taxis are a quick, easy and affordable way to get around. Even the beaches south of the city aren't too expensive if you're in a hurry and don't want to take a bus.

You can hail taxis from the street, but it's safer to call a taxi service to have one pick you up. This can be done through your hostel or hotel's reception desk, as well as at nicer restaurants. Upon calling, they will give you a code to confirm with the driver, thereby ensuring you're getting in the right taxi.

And of course there are web-based services such as Uber and Easy Taxi.

Learn the rules of taking taxis in Peru in the previous chapter.

By Bus

Travelers on a shoestring will not want to take taxis everywhere they go. Traditional public transportation in Peru is a confusing system of private buses known as "combis" or "micros" (pictured at the beginning of chapter) which shuttle people around the city. Some are large, some are tiny. Almost all are dilapidated and drive aggressively.

Destinations are posted in the windshields and on the side of the bus. It's important to know exactly where a bus goes because these buses don't stay on only one street. A typical route can turn several times, and drivers are known to leave their route to avoid traffic.

Combis can sometimes be hailed anywhere, but only at designated bus stops on the major thoroughfares. Look for the street signs. The fare will vary by route and how far you're going, but the average is about 1 sol. Once you hail your combi, enter through the side door and find a seat. If there are no seats, which is common, squeeze into a space and grab a hand rail.

Watch the streets so you know when you're close to your destination. When you're ready to get off, call out "Baja." This tells the driver to let you off. Pay the "cobrador," a second bus employee responsible for collecting fares, and hop off quickly before the bus tears off again. If you aren't sure how to recognize your destination, tell the cobrador where you're going and he'll let you know the best place to get off.

Taking combis in Peru is pretty easy to learn, but we only recommend it for experienced Latin American travelers. It doesn't cost much more to take a safe taxi or the Metropolitano bus system, where there's no chance you'll be left in the middle of an unknown neighborhood with no idea where to go.

By Corredor Azul

Since the first edition of this guide, the city of Lima has implemented the Integrated System of Transportation (SIT) to modernize the chaotic bus network. These larger, better-maintained and cleaner buses only pick up and drop off at designated stops along fixed routes.

The system of Corredores (corridors), as they're known, managed to remove many of the ancient and informal buses from the thoroughfares with the heaviest traffic, but poor planning resulted in insufficient supply so they are always crowded. If time is a concern, they should be avoided altogether during rush hour. Still, international visitors may be more comfortable taking these buses over the combis.

The city initially color-coded the routes, with the Corredor Azul (blue) running Arequipa Avenue from Miraflores all the way downtown, the Corredor Rojo (red) going from La Molina in the east along Javier Prado avenue to Callao and the Corredor Morado (purple) in the low-income districts of San Juan de Lurigancho and Rimac.

Unfortunately, the city's false starts, voided contracts and reshuffling of the plan have put blue buses on other routes, prompting the media to call the entire system "Corredor Azul." But if you try to look up the information online, you'll just get confused with the red and purple lines, so don't take the colors seriously.

At the time of this writing, the city transport authority and Peru's newspapers are denoting each specific route as "Tacna-Garcilaso-Arequipa" and "Javier Prado-La Marina-Faucett" for the names of the route's avenues instead of "Blue Corridor" and "Red Corridor."

To take a Corredor, find a bus stop on the route marked by a blue "Paradero" street sign. A transportation employee will often be posted at the stop to organize the line and collect fares before the bus arrives. If not, you can pay the bus driver 1.50 soles upon boarding.

When taking a Tacna-Garcilaso-Arequipa Corredor bus from downtown or Lince toward Miraflores, pay close attention to the route number on the bus. The 306 stops in San Isidro before Miraflores. And only the 301 goes all the way to Barranco.

Likewise on the Javier Prado-La Marina-Faucett route, make sure you are on a 201 if you need to go to Parque de las Leyendas or further west into San Miguel, or the 209 if you're going to the Catholic University or San Marcos National University.

When in doubt, ask the attendant or bus driver before paying your fare. Because this system is brand new and constantly subject to change and improvisation, they're used to questions.

By Metropolitano

Lima has a Metropolitano bus-rapid transit (BRT) system of natural gas-powered, articulated buses with elevated platform stations in dedicated lanes. Rechargeable cards cost 4.50 soles ($1), with a single trip costing 2.50 soles. Taking the Metropolitano will be more like taking a subway for Westerners.

The Metropolitano has only one route connecting from Comas in the far north to Chorrillos in the south. There are stops in Miraflores, San Isidro, Barranco and downtown.

These buses travel in dedicated lanes, which save passengers time by skipping traffic. Wait times are usually minimal, with buses arriving every five to 10 minutes. But like the Corredores, the Metropolitano gets so crowded at peak times that it should be avoided during rush hour unless you're prepared to squeeze in like a sardine.

While the BRT buses do not wait for traffic, the locations of Metropolitano stations and the time getting in and out of the stations make combis and Corredores faster for short trips. The Metropolitano was designed for Lima residents going long distances.

But with stations just a couple blocks from Miraflores' Parque Kennedy and Barranco's Parque Municipal, the Metropolitano is an easier way for tourists to take public transportation to the historic city center and avoid the confusion and possible mistakes on combis or Corredores.

Below is a list of useful stations:

- La Colmena: one block from Plaza San Martin in the heart of the historic city center.
- Estacion Central: underground terminal close to Parque de la Exposicion, Real Plaza shopping mall and the Palacio de Justicia (the starting point for this guide's Downtown Lima Walking Tour).
- Canaval y Moreyra: serves Lima's financial district in San Isidro.
- Ricardo Palma: closest station to Parque Kennedy in Miraflores.
- Benavides: closest station to Larco Avenue in Miraflores.
- 28 de Julio: closest station to Larcomar and the Malecon in Miraflores.
- Bulevar: closest station to Parque Municipal and the heart of Barranco.

The A bus which you probably won't need runs from downtown to the working-class districts in the north, ending in Independencia. The C bus runs the tourist beat from Chorillos to downtown. The B bus runs the entire line.

Numbered buses are express routes which skip some stations to save time. To avoid errors, stick to the letters. Only take Expresos when you've learned which stops they serve and at what times on which days.

For more information about the Metropolitano's feeder buses, pictures, a full list of stations and detailed descriptions, see goo.gl/ZqPCbF.

By Metro

In 2012, Lima inaugurated the Metro de Lima, a light-rail train commonly known as the "tren electrico." At the time of publish there is only one line in service, but it's going to be sweet when they expand it to five. A second line currently under construction will serve the airport. Slated for 2018, it will connect to the Estacion Central Metropolitano station downtown, allowing tourists to take public transportation from the airport to the tourist areas of Miraflores, Barranco and San Isidro.

Like the Metropolitano, the aim of the Metro's first line was to provide mobility to Lima's lower classes who live in districts far from central Lima, and whose commutes ran two to three hours each way. With the Metro, residents of San Juan de Lurigancho and Villa El Salvador can arrive in central Lima in a fraction of the time it took before.

But in its current form, the Metro does not serve areas international visitors and foreign residents will ever go. There are stations in Surco and San Borja. But even if you live or work near those stations, there aren't many places you would take it to.

The Grau station is a short walk from downtown Lima. But while it looks close on a map, the direct route from the station to the city center goes through Barrios Altos, one of Lima's most notorious neighborhoods for crime. If you want to take the Metro downtown, be aware that Grau Avenue is the kind of place where even

Peruvians get robbed.

The Gamarra station is located in Lima's historic garment district. It would be hard to lose your way, but be careful just in case or you could get lost in La Victoria. The Gamarra station does have a shuttle bus you can take to the Estacion Central Metropolitano station in downtown Lima.

The Cultura station is located in Lima's top convention district, home to the Lima Convention Center, Grand National Theater, National Library and Museum of the Nation. But if coming from San Borja or Surco, it's just not far enough to warrant a train ride.

Metro feeder buses serve Barranco and Chorrillos as well as various low-income neighborhoods in the southern outskirts.

The metro runs between 6 a.m. and 10 p.m. daily. To use the Metro, you have to purchase a rechargeable card for 5 soles ($1.50). Once you have the card, each trip costs 1.50 soles.

Unlike the Corredores and Metropolitano, the Metro isn't crowded only during rush hour. It's jam-packed every day.

Chapter 7
Neighborhoods

The City of Kings was founded in what is now downtown Lima. Central Lima spans from the Plaza de Armas to Pueblo Libre in the west, San Isidro in the south and La Victoria in the east. The most popular neighborhoods among tourists and foreign residents are the southern districts of Miraflores, Barranco and Surco.

On the west side of Lima is the constitutional province of Callao, where the international airport and South America's largest Pacific seaport are located. While it is administered separately, Callao forms part of the Lima metropolitan area.

The northern half of the metropolitan area is almost entirely working class of little interest to most tourists, with the exception of the Rimac opposite the Rimac River from the historic city center.

To the north and south of Lima are coastal towns and beaches. East of the mountains are touristic pueblos which enjoy sunshine during the Lima winter.

We cannot cover each of metropolitan Lima's three dozen districts. Below are the most relevant for international visitors.

CERCADO

Cercado is the name of Lima's downtown district. "Cercado" means "fenced," and it gets its name from the walls which protected the city from attack for over 200 years until they were torn down to allow expansion in the 19th century.

A UNESCO World Heritage Site, Lima's historic city center features plazas, government buildings and colonial churches. While there are areas with prostitution and drugs and walking late at night can be dangerous, Lima's city center is safer than most other Latin American capitals.

The Viceroyalty of Peru was the capital of Spanish South America for over 200 years. While Mexico City governed Central America and the Caribbean, Spain ruled over its South American territories from Lima. So there is an abundance of historic sites to visit including churches and cathedrals, museums, colonial houses and more.

While the heart of Lima's nightlife has moved to southern Lima near the coast, there are interesting bars and restaurants downtown as well.

Points of Interest:

- Plaza de Armas
- Plaza San Martin
- Parque de la Exposicion
- Parque de la Reserva
- Congress
- Palace of Justice
- Barrio Chino (Chinatown)
- Alameda Chabuca Granda
- Estadio Nacional

MIRAFLORES

If you're staying in Lima, chances are you'll stay in Miraflores. The district is one of the most beautiful, cleanest and safest parts of Lima. Originally a beach community outside the city, Miraflores has emerged as the heart of tourism, dining and entertainment.

Miraflores is home to modern shopping malls and the city's best hotels and restaurants. It also boasts the most backpacker hostels. Bars, restaurants and dance clubs are centered around Parque Kennedy. One of the city's most emblematic images, the Larcomar shopping mall, is built into the side of a cliff overlooking the Pacific Ocean.

Points of Interest:

- Parque Kennedy
- Calle de las Pizzas
- Huaca Pucllana ruins
- Larcomar
- Malecon boardwalk
- Parque del Amor
- La Marina lighthouse

For more information, visit limacitykings.com/miraflores.

SAN ISIDRO

San Isidro, located just north of Miraflores, is the financial center of Lima. The commercial district west of the Via Expresa highway is home to the country's top banks and largest companies' headquarters.

The historic Lima Golf Club, pristine Parque El Olivar and luxury shopping on Conquistadores Avenue give an unmistakable air of economic elite. Corporate high rises give way to high-end dining and upper-class residences overlooking public parks with litter-free, manicured lawns.

While the party crowd will be attracted to Miraflores or Barranco, the more mature travelers and those in Lima on business will prefer San Isidro.

Points of Interest:

- Parque El Olivar
- Huaca Huallamarca ruins
- Lima financial district
- American Chamber of Commerce

For more information, visit limacitykings.com/san-isidro.

BARRANCO

Barranco is a bohemian neighborhood south of Miraflores popular for its artistic charm. Home to hostels, restaurants and dance clubs, many international visitors choose Barranco as a more romantic alternative to the foreigner-dense Miraflores.

A short walk will see colonial and republican mansions – both preserved and abandoned – and modern apartment buildings overlooking the Pacific Ocean. Barranco is home to a formidable nightlife which draws singles from all over Lima.

Barranco is tucked along the coast and out of the way of most commutes. While life in Lima can generally be characterized by blaring car horns and roaring buses, Barranco is one of a few places where you can enjoy a fairly quiet life. The downside of that, however, is that it's not the most convenient area if you need to commute further than the typical tourist beat.

Points of Interest:

- Puente de Suspiros (Bridge of Sighs)
- La Ermita chapel
- Parque Municipal
- Boulevard Sanchez Carrion
- Paseo Saenz Peña

For more information, visit limacitykings.com/barranco.

SURCO

The Santiago de Surco district, known simply as "Surco," is an upscale district with a more suburban layout than Miraflores or San Isidro. Urban development came later than the rest of the city, which resulted in more sprawl, more room for parks and pricier real estate.

While Surco is mostly off the beaten path for tourists, it is a popular choice of residence for Lima's upper classes precisely because it is out of the way. Surco is home to one of Lima's best parks in Parque de la Amistad (Friendship Park) and the main square hosts Lima's annual wine and pisco festival. Surco is also home to Peru's trendiest shopping malls, four of Lima's best universities and the U.S.

embassy.
Points of Interest:

- Plaza de Armas de Surco
- Parque de la Amistad
- Parque Ecologico Loma Amarilla
- Jockey Plaza shopping mall
- U.S. embassy

For more information, visit limacitykings.com/surco.

CHORRILLOS

Chorrillos is just south of Barranco along the Pacific Coast. The district is the closest thing to a beach community in Lima because of its sand, as opposed to the rocky shores that line most of the city. However the crowds and stagnant water will be a turnoff for most beach bums.

Despite the crowded beach, Chorrillos is worth a visit for the fish market at the pier. There you can find day-fresh ceviche for the best price in the city. Haku Tours (www.hakutours.com) offers guided tours of the market.

Points of Interest:

- Morro Solar
- Terminal de Chorrillos fish market
- Agua Dulce beach

LINCE

Lince, where I've lived since 2013, is a tiny district just south of the city center, conveniently located near anywhere in the city. A short walk from the financial district in San Isidro, many of Lima's best restaurants establish themselves in Lince to take advantage of more affordable rent while being close to the workplaces of white-collar professionals.

At night, Arequipa Avenue comes alive as a popular nightlife spot for middle-class Peruvians. In case you're looking to party off the beaten path of Miraflores and Barranco, you won't see many tourists in these dance clubs. Lince is also where you'll find the after-hours bars.

Bordered to the east by La Victoria, late-night walks in parts of Lince come with an edgier vibe.

Points of Interest:

- Parque Mariscal Ramon Castilla

JESUS MARIA

Just west of Lince, Jesus Maria is a middle- to upper-middle-class area of beautifully-preserved, colonial-style houses which often sit next to modern, high-rise apartment buildings.

Home to Campo de Marte, Parque de los Proceres (which contains an ice-skating rink) and the central plaza in Parque Caceres, Jesus Maria is one of the more accessible middle-class districts in central Lima. It is also home to several government ministries, foreign embassies, the venerable University of the Pacific and more.

Points of Interest:

- Campo de Marte
- Parque de los Proceres
- Barrio Japones (Japanese Town)
- Lima Chamber of Commerce

PUEBLO LIBRE

Pueblo Libre, or Free Town, owes its name to being the temporary home of the continental independence fighter, Simon Bolivar. It was later made a "reduccion," where Peruvian Indians were concentrated from their dispersed rural homes into urban centers to accustom them to city life and facilitate conversion to Christianity.

The middle-class district has retained the feel of an old village, as have other reduccion neighborhoods. Pueblo Libre is home to two of Peru's most important museums in the Larco Museum and the National Museum of Archaeology, Anthropology and History of Peru. In its central square, Plaza Bolivar, you'll find some of Lima's better gastronomy and nightlife. Yet the district as a whole remains quiet.

Points of Interest:

- Plaza Bolivar

SAN BORJA

San Borja, formerly a part of Surco, is similar in being an upper-class area with a more suburban sprawl and plenty of green space. It is home to pre-Inca archaeological ruins, Huaca San Borja and Huaca Limatambo, as well as many of Peru's government ministries and the Lima Convention Center.

Another of Lima's largest green spaces in Pentagonito, a military base, is located in San Borja. Every Sunday the park hosts various sports for families.

Points of Interest:

- Lima Convention Center
- Grand National Theater
- National Library
- Huaca San Borja and Huaca Limatambo
- Pentagonito

LA MOLINA

La Molina is an upper-class, suburban district at the far east of the city. While Miraflores and San Isidro are upscale, La Molina is Lima's most exclusive district, home to many of Peru's celebrities, politicians and wealthy families because it affords privacy. In addition, La Molina is home to many American expats who made the leap to Peru but aren't willing to give up the suburban lifestyle of quiet neighborhoods and ample green spaces.

However, you almost have to own a car to live in La Molina. If you're coming to Lima for tourism and don't have a resident friend in La Molina to drive you around every day, stay somewhere else.

DANGEROUS DISTRICTS

While Lima is safer than most Latin American capitals, Peru has a history of extreme inequality, grinding poverty and indiscriminate violence. There are districts to avoid.

Some of the dangerous districts were great neighborhoods long ago. Callao is home to the beautiful La Punta district, a recommended tourist attraction in this guide. Some travelers are interested in seeing the neighborhoods below the poverty line which, according to government data, over half of Peruvians live in. A shantytown tour is another recommended thing to do in Lima.

La Victoria is home to the Gamarra garment district, and Rimac is home to the oldest bullring in the Americas, San Cerro Cristobal and the Convent of the Barefoot Carmelites museum.

While many of Lima's cultural gems are located in low-income neighborhoods, below is a list of areas to avoid if you don't want to take any risk whatsoever.

- Ate
- Barrios Altos
- Callao
- Carabayllo
- Comas
- El Agustino
- Independencia
- La Victoria
- Los Olivos
- Puente Piedra
- Rimac
- San Juan de Lurigancho
- San Juan de Miraflores
- San Luis
- San Martin de Porres
- Santa Anita
- Villa El Salvador
- Villa Maria del Triunfo

Chapter 8
Where to Stay

Most tourist accommodations are located in Miraflores, within walking distance of Parque Kennedy and the Larcomar mall.

HOSTELS

The overall quality of hostels in Lima is on par with what you'll find in other Latin American capitals like Mexico City and Buenos Aires. It's not great, but the locations are convenient and the dorm beds will be far cheaper than any hotel in the area.

Costs can go up significantly for private rooms, which can make getting a room in a budget hotel an equally if not more affordable option. For safety reasons, most hostels and many cheap hotels have policies against allowing visitors in the rooms.

1900 Backpackers Hostel
Av. Garcilaso de la Vega 1588, Cercado
www.1900hostel.com

If you prefer to stay in downtown Lima, this hostel housed in a recently renovated mansion has you covered. The central location puts you across the street from Parque de la Exposicion and within walking distance of the historic city center, Magic Water Circuit and countless museums.

Backpackers Family House
Cl. Juan Moore 304, Miraflores
www.backpackersfamilyhouse.com

This homey hostel was rated the best hostel in Peru on Hostelworld in 2008 and 2009, and continues to receive praise from backpackers. While only a block from the Malecon boardwalk and beaches, it's about 10 blocks west of Parque Kennedy and 15 blocks from the Larcomar mall.

Barranco's Backpacker Inn
Malecon Castilla 260, Barranco
www.barrancobackpackersperu.com

Barranco is known for being a bit cheaper than Miraflores, and that goes for the hostels too. Barranco's Backpacker Inn is the most popular option.

Dragonfly Hostels
Av. 28 de Julio 190, Miraflores
www.dragonflyhostels.com

Dragonfly is centrally located in Miraflores and brews its own beer, which it serves on the rooftop terrace. Dragonfly has two more locations in Cusco and Arequipa.

Flying Dog Hostel
Av. Diez Canseco 117, Miraflores
www.flyingdogperu.com

The Flying Dog Hostel began in Lima back in 2000, and has since grown to three locations in Miraflores, two in Cusco, and one each in Arequipa and Iquitos. One location above the popular La Lucha Sangucheria restaurant has a view of Parque Kennedy across the street.

Hostelling International
Av. Casimiro Ulloa 328, Miraflores
www.hihostels.com

If you're looking for a hostel that's required to meet specific standards of quality, then you can always count on Hostelling International. But the quality comes at a cost, with dorm beds starting at almost twice the price of the cheapest beds in the city.

Kaminu Backpackers Hostel
Bajada de Baños 342, Barranco
www.kaminu.com

Located in the Bajada de Baños pathway leading to the beach, this hostel sits under Barranco's signature landmark, the Puente de Suspiros bridge. The rooftop kitchen and bar makes it my favorite for the quiet nights relaxing to the smell of the sea. Prices are moderate and the proprietor, Piero, treats everyone like family. This is also a good place to practice your Spanish as it's more of a favorite among Latin travelers.

Pariwana Backpacker Hostels
Av. Larco 189, Miraflores
www.pariwana-hostel.com

Pariwana is the rare party hostel that also manages to receive consistently high ratings. Located across the street from Parque Kennedy, it features a decent breakfast, bar, TV room and rooftop terrace.

Red Psycho Llama Eco Hostel
Cl. Colina 183, Miraflores
www.redpsychollama.hostel.com

A block from Parque Kennedy, this is a smaller hostel with an ecotourism theme.

HOTELS

In addition to attracting tourists from around the world, Lima hosts a substantial number of business travelers and is positioning itself as South America's top convention city. It has a huge selection of hotels ranging from five-star luxury to boutique and more value-oriented options.

Hotel Antigua Miraflores
Av. Grau 350, Miraflores
www.antiguamiraflores.com

Antigua Miraflores is a mid-range hotel with the look and feel of a bed and breakfast. It's housed in a recently renovated, pink mansion located in central Miraflores. It's five blocks to Parque Kennedy, ten blocks to Larcomar.

Hotel Atton San Isidro
Av. Jorge Basadre 595, San Isidro
sanisidro.atton.com

Since it opened in 2011, this 252-room hotel has consistently ranked as one of the top hotels in Lima on TripAdvisor. The San Isidro location puts you in the heart of the business and financial district of Lima, and leaves you a short taxi ride away from the beaches and nightlife of Miraflores.

B Arts Boutique Hotel
Av. Prol. San Martin 301, Barranco
hotelb.pe

Located in a white Belle Epoque-style mansion on the elegant Paseo Saenz Peña promenade in the heart of Barranco, the B Arts Boutique Hotel exudes sophistication and is regularly drooled over in international newspapers. In 2014, the hotel will celebrate its 100th anniversary.

Casa Andina Classic - Miraflores San Antonio
Cl. Schell 452, Miraflores
www.casa-andina.com

Fully renovated in 2011, Casa Andina is a mid-range hotel located in a quieter area of Miraflores. It's a 10-minute walk from Larcomar and the beach. The Casa Andina chain has four high-end hotels in Miraflores.

Gran Hotel Bolivar
Jr. de la Union 958, Cercado
www.granhotelbolivar.com.pe

Built in 1924, the Gran Hotel Bolivar was Lima's first modern hotel. It was the accommodation of choice for celebrities including Orson Welles, Ava Gardner and John Wayne. The Rolling Stones were once kicked out for bad behavior. Pictured at the beginning of this chapter, the hotel is located downtown in Plaza San Martin.

Hotel Maury
Jr. Ucayali 201, Cercado

Hotel Maury is located one block from the Plaza de Armas in downtown Lima. The hotel bar, Bar Maury, is where the pisco sour was invented in the early 1900s when an American guest asked for a whiskey sour, but the bartender had no whiskey.

JW Marriott Hotel Lima
Malecon de la Reserva 165, Miraflores
www.marriott.com

Across the street from the Larcomar shopping center with views of the Pacific Ocean, the JW Marriott is widely recognized as the finest hotel in Lima.

Hotel Milan
Jr. Bartolome Herrera 364, Lince

In Lince there is a district of budget hotels on and around Petit Thouars Avenue. If you prefer to be off the beaten path and far from other tourists, this area is great for a private room. Hotel Milan is just one example in the area. Most of the options don't have websites, so you just have to show up and request a room.
Be warned that many hotels around here are used by couples who want to be alone but still live with their parents. If a hotel offers hourly rates, be warned what the neighbors will be doing at night.

Runcu Hotel
Av. de la Aviacion 139, Miraflores
www.hotelruncu.com

Situated a few blocks from the beach, Runcu Hotel is a budget-friendly hotel that offers free breakfast and Wi-Fi. While it's blocks from Parque Kennedy and 15 blocks from Larcomar, it is one of few locations in Miraflores within one block from a pathway leading down the cliffs to the beach.

Swissotel Lima
Av. Santo Toribio 173, San Isidro
www.swissotel.com

The Swissotel Lima is a business-oriented luxury hotel featuring five restaurants, including La Locanda for Peruvian food, La Fondue for Swiss and European food and Sushi Cage if you're in the mood for Japanese. Located in the San Isidro financial district, it is one of few which could claim the title of best hotel in Lima.

The Westin Lima Hotel & Convention Center
Cl. Las Begonias 450, San Isidro
www.starwoodhotels.com

At 30 stories, the modern and luxurious Westin Lima Hotel was the tallest building in Peru before the new state bank headquarters was built in 2015. The Westin facilities include a spa, indoor pool, and fitness center, in addition to the convention center implied in the name. Again, arguably the best hotel in Lima and located in the financial district.

SHORT-TERM ROOMS AND APARTMENTS

If you plan to spend a week or more in the city, consider renting a room or apartment. Furnished apartments within a five- to 10-minute walk of Parque Kennedy in Miraflores can be had for as little as $500 per month. Just a room can be had for as little as $150. More economic options can be found in central Lima.

Whatever room or apartment you consider taking, always try to negotiate for a lower price. That doesn't mean everybody will come down, but you have to try.

Airbnb

Airbnb features hundreds of room and apartment rentals. The trend of buying real estate and making the mortgage payment by renting to Airbnb customers has definitely arrived in Lima, so there are ample options of homeowners-turned-hoteliers vying for your business.

Craigslist

Craigslist features a mix of listings by owners as well as third-party rental agencies. It'll take you time to weed through the duplicates, but it's another resource for finding a place to stay.

El Comercio

Pick up a copy of the Sunday edition of this newspaper to check for listings in Urbania, the residential classifieds. Or check the website at urbania.pe, where the listings may be a little less reliable than the print edition. Given El Comercio is a Spanish-language newspaper whose classifieds are aimed at locals, these prices are the least likely on this list to be inflated for foreigners. They don't have many short-term rentals, but it's worth a try.

Living in Peru classifieds

Living in Peru is Peru's most popular English-language website. It receives a steady dose of classifieds which, while expensive and almost entirely located within Miraflores, are worth a look at peruthisweek.com/classifieds/housing.

Couchsurfing

Couchsurfing in Lima is the old standard to save money while seeing the city through a friendly native's eyes. Because many Peruvians live with their parents until marriage, it may be hard to find a place where you're not also living with a full family. Tap into the community by joining the Couchsurfing group for Lima, or inviting members out for coffee or a drink.

Chapter 9
The Five Best Museums

CATHEDRAL OF LIMA

Catedral de Lima
Jiron Carabaya s/n
Hours: Monday through Friday 9 a.m. to 5 p.m., Saturdays 10 a.m. to 1 p.m.
Admission: 10 soles ($3)
www.facebook.com/museo.catedral.de.lima

The founding and history of Lima were always linked with the Catholic Church. The role of religion was so great that visiting Peru's museums will inevitably lead you to churches and religious art. The historic city center has dozens of churches, three of which are home to notable museums. Of those three, the Cathedral of Lima is the most impressive.

Located in the Plaza de Armas, the Cathedral represents Lima in Peru's Wealth and Pride collectors' coins as its most iconic image. It is also home to the tomb of Spanish conquistador, Francisco Pizarro (pictured above).

Intricate stonework on the façade depicts Jesus and the apostles just below Peru's coat of arms. Inside is a grandiose sanctuary with a gold-plated altar flanked by wooden choir stalls. Running along the sides of the church are 14 chapel altars dedicated to various saints. At the back is the museum of religious art which features paintings, sculptures, vestments and more.

The first edition of this guide featured San Francisco Museum in this list because it consistently ranks as international tourists' favorite. However the 70,000 skeletons in the church's basement which served as a graveyard for over 100 years, the main attraction, may be scary for children. If you're more into dungeons and skulls than religious art, the San Francisco Catacombs and Museum on Ancash Street just east of the Government Palace may be for you.

For those who don't want a long tour of religious art or dungeons, the Santo Domingo Convent on Camana Street west of the Government Palace is a quick and easy tour of beautiful courtyards and chapels lighter on the art galleries.

REAL FELIPE FORTRESS

Fortaleza Real Felipe
Plaza Independencia s/n, Callao
Hours: 9 a.m. to 4 p.m.
Admission: 15 soles ($4) for tourists
www.realfelipe.com

The Real Felipe Fortress was built in the 18th century to defend the port of Callao from pirates and amphibian invasions. The fortress was later used by Spanish loyalists to defend against patriot armies looking to liberate Peru. In its peak of glory, cannons reinforcing Peru's navy repelled a Spanish invasion in the Chincha Islands War of 1866.

The fortress has been converted into a military and history museum. Essentially an 18th-century castle, the structure itself is worth a visit. Inside are 19th-century cannons, tanks from World War II, Peru's military uniforms over the ages, a house telling the story of a fallen hero from the War of the Pacific against Chile and, of course, pirates. Live actors tell some of the stories.

This is one of Lima's least-visited attractions, which I attribute to its location in Callao. It's not convenient to get to, but more importantly Callao is a mostly low-income area which Peruvians don't promote. I've never had a problem in all the times I've visited. And in my opinion, it's the best museum in Lima.

If you're a military history buff, make it a sweet day with a visit to Peru's Naval Museum one block away.

MALI LIMA ART MUSEUM

MALI Museo de Arte de Lima
Paseo Colon 125, Lima
Hours: Tuesday to Friday 10 a.m. to 7 p.m., Saturday and Sunday 10 a.m. to 5 p.m.
Admission: 30 soles ($9)
www.mali.pe

The MALI art museum is Peru's most important art collection. A cultural icon in Lima, MALI has more than 17,000 pieces spanning over 3,000 years of Peruvian history including pre-Columbian, colonial, republican and modern eras.

The museum displays so much that it would take an entire day, or a return visit, to see it all. A more pedestrian walk-through could be done in a few hours, but somebody looking to read the context and explanations of each piece, and especially Peruvian history enthusiasts, would need at least a full day for MALI.

The MALI art museum is located in a 19th-century palace in Parque de la Exposicion, just south of the historic city center.

NATIONAL MUSEUM OF ARCHAEOLOGY, ANTHROPOLOGY AND HISTORY OF PERU

Museo Nacional de Arqueologia, Antropologia e Historia del Peru
Plaza Bolivar, Pueblo Libre
Hours: Tuesday to Saturday 9 a.m. to 5 p.m., Sundays and Holidays 9 a.m. to 4 p.m.
Admission: 10 soles ($3)
mnaahp.cultura.pe

The National Museum of Archaeology, Anthropology and History of Peru, managed by the Peruvian government's Ministry of Culture, is the most important history museum in Peru.

The museum features exhibits from pre-Columbian cultures, the colonial period and the republican age. Everything from portraits and metal works to topography models depict the national character.

The highlights of this museum are the curiously deformed Paracas skulls, Paracas textiles, topography models of Inca architecture and architectural models of Lima during the colonial era. This is also the best museum to visit to get a deeper grasp of Peru's trajectory from colony to independence than the first chapter of this guide gives.

Located just one mile from the Larco Museum in Pueblo Libre, an ambitious educational agenda could visit both museums in one day.

LARCO MUSEUM

Museo Larco
Av. Bolivar 1515, Pueblo Libre
Hours: 9 a.m. to 10 p.m.
Admission: 30 soles ($9)
www.museolarco.org

Rafael Larco was an early-20th-century historian whose obsession led him to collect thousands of artifacts from Peru's pre-Columbian cultures. The elegant building and garden illustrate how to deliver beauty under Lima's gray skies, and the museum also features an excellent restaurant.

Larco is credited with discovering the Moche Culture, which produced the museum's claim to fame: a gallery dedicated to erotic pottery with clay figures of couples engaged in various sexual positions. Also from the Mochicas is an exhibit explaining their human-sacrifice and cannibalism rituals.

All of the travel websites and English-language media consider Larco Museum the city's best museum, something I vehemently disagree with. I certainly include it in the top five, but I think that it would never be mentioned without the erotic pottery. And even with it, I put it last on this list.

Chapter 10
Ten Things to Do in Lima

These are our 10 most recommended tourist activities in Lima.

1. DOWNTOWN LIMA WALKING TOUR

Lima's city center is one of the most magnificent and historically significant among Latin America's capitals. Downtown Lima is safe during the day, and visiting at night is safe if you are reasonably careful.

Points of interest:

- Plaza de Armas: Government Palace, Cathedral of Lima, Archbishop's Palace, Municipal Palace of Lima
- Plaza San Martin
- Plaza Grau: Justice Palace and Casa Roosevelt
- San Francisco Basilica and Convent (pictured)
- Plaza Francia and Recoleta Church
- Alameda Chabuca Granda and the perennially closed Parque de la Muralla
- Congress
- Parque Universitario and Plaza de la Cultura
- San Pedro Basilica and Convent
- La Merced Church
- Torre Tagle Palace
- Jiron de la Union
- Camana Avenue churches: Santo Domingo Convent, San Agustin Church

and Jesus Maria and Jose Monastery
- Tacna Avenue churches: Santa Rosa, San Sebastian, Iglesia de las Nazarenas and San Marcelo
- Barrio Chino
- Paseo Colon

All the tourism agencies offer guided tours of the historic city center. For a less involved tour, take a taxi or bus to the Plaza de Armas where double-decker buses are constantly offering tours.

To take a tour without a guide, see my recommended walking tour with custom Google Map, pictures and detailed instructions at limacitykings.com/downtown-lima-walking-tour.

While the city center is safe, like any big city it borders less-than-safe areas. Here are some borders to avoid sketchier neighborhoods:
1. Do not cross any bridges over the Rimac River.
2. Do not go south of Grau Avenue.
3. Do not go west of Tacna Avenue.
4. Do not cross Abancay Avenue going east. The first couple blocks to see Barrio Chino or the National School of Fine Arts shouldn't be a problem, but no further.

2. MIRAFLORES WALKING TOUR

Miraflores is Lima's heart of tourism, entertainment and leisure. Known for shopping, gardens, parks and beaches, Miraflores is Lima's best-known upscale district.

Below are the best sites to see within walking distance of Parque Kennedy and Larcomar:
- Parque Kennedy
- Calle de las Pizzas
- Larcomar
- Malecon

- Parque del Amor
- Parque Salazar
- La Marina lighthouse
- Parque Reducto No. 2
- Parque Las Tradiciones

For a suggested tour which passes most of the sites above with a custom Google Map of the route embedded as well as detailed instructions with pictures, visit limacitykings.com/miraflores-walking-tour.

Miraflores is completely safe. No borders to be careful of. Feel free to get lost exploring.

3. BARRANCO WALKING TOUR

Barranco is a bohemian, beachside community just south of Miraflores. Where Miraflores is hustle, bustle and business, Barranco has a more laidback, artistic vibe.

Points of interest in Barranco:

- Parque Municipal de Barranco: Barranco library, Santisima Cruz Church
- Boulevard Sanchez Carrion
- Paseo Saenz Peña promenade
- La Ermita chapel
- Puente de los Suspiros bridge
- Bajada de Baños

For a custom-designed walking tour of Barranco with instructions and pictures, visit limacitykings.com/barranco-walking-tour.

Most of Barranco is safe. There is a small area which is sketchy, but you won't come near it if you stay within seven or eight blocks from the coastline.

4. LA PUNTA DEL CALLAO

All the foreign tourists to Lima inevitably visit Miraflores, Barranco and the city center. Unfortunately, the vast majority do not visit La Punta.

While Callao is listed among our Dangerous Districts, La Punta del Callao is an upscale oasis which offers history, architecture, naval culture, rocky beaches, seafood and luxurious residential streets.

Callao is legally a "constitutional province" spanning 57 square miles with a population of over 1 million. Callao is home to the largest Pacific seaport in South America and the Lima international airport. The reputation for poverty and crime comes from the vast low-income areas outside La Punta.

To get in or out, you have to pass through much of Callao. But it is generally safe to travel the main avenues during the day, and it's worth the trip.

The taxis drop you off at Plaza Grau because it costs extra to enter La Punta. The plaza features a dock overlooking the seaport's first terminal of shipping containers, where you can take a motorized boat tour of the port and La Punta.

Walk west toward La Punta from Plaza Grau, or keep the sea on your right. You will immediately come across the Real Felipe Fortress, which was built to defend Lima from pirates and is now one of Lima's best museums. Continue down the avenue to enter Chucuito, a neighborhood originally settled by Italian-Peruvians that buffers old Callao from La Punta.

The walk from Plaza Grau and Real Felipe Fortress to the entrance of La Punta is about one mile. To skip Chucuito and the walking, hail any combi bus to ride in. It's impossible to get lost in La Punta, a peninsula 11 blocks long and three blocks wide.

Whether walking or riding, you'll pass the Peruvian Navy lighthouse and the SUNAT customs office before reaching Plaza Galvez, the entrance to La Punta. Beyond Plaza Galvez you'll see pristine streets, republican mansions and a recreational boating culture.

On the north coast of La Punta is Playa Cantolao beach. The beaches in La Punta are rocky, but some people will swim on this side. On the south is a manicured green space, Malecon Wiese, which features a pedestrian path and distant views of the Lima coast.

Nearing the end of the peninsula is Plaza Matriz, the main plaza of the La Punta district. Behind the square is the Peruvian Naval Academy. At the tip of the peninsula, beyond the last houses, is Plaza San Martin, a public area with benches, a skate park and an excellent looking point. There are also plenty of restaurants. If you didn't take a boat tour near the port of Callao, you can catch one here, but it won't be motorized.

In the distance are San Lorenzo and El Fronton islands. Pirates including Sir Francis Drake used San Lorenzo to stage attacks on ships coming and going from Callao, while El Fronton was home to a now-shuttered prison like Alcatraz.

Old Callao

Back where the taxi drops off next to the seaport is the historic center of Callao. Across the avenue and stoplight from Plaza Grau are deteriorated buildings that haven't seen upkeep in years. Some seem to be falling down. The area is improving, but it can be dangerous according to locals.

Just two blocks from the port is the Iglesia Matriz plaza, home to some great ceviche restaurants which offer good value. The refurbished Casa Ronald hosts art galleries, fine restaurants and even a brewpub.

For a more ecological experience, you can take a boat tour from Plaza Grau to the tiny Palomino Islands between San Lorenzo and El Fronton. Visitors can swim with the penguins, sea lions and seabirds (whose valuable guano gives off a strong smell) which inhabit the islands.

Points of interest in La Punta and nearby Callao:

- Port of Callao
- Real Felipe Fortress
- Plaza Galvez
- Plaza Matriz
- Plaza San Martin
- Malecon Wiese boardwalk
- Playa Cantolao
- Palomino Islands

For more information with a custom Google Map, visit limacitykings.com/punta-callao.

5. MAGIC WATER CIRCUIT

Circuito Magico del Agua
Jr. Madre de Dios s/n, Cercado
Hours: 3 p.m. to 10:30 p.m. Closed on Mondays except holidays.
Admission: 4 soles ($1)
www.circuitomagicodelagua.com.pe

The Magic Water Circuit in Parque de la Reserva has been verified by the Guinness Book of World Records as the world's largest fountain complex in a public park. It consists of 13 water fountains that combine music, colored lights and laser effects for a family-friendly must-see in Lima. Even if you don't have children, the Magic Water Circuit is a cheap date or just something to do while people-watching.

Some fountains are interactive, with names like Tunnel of Surprises, Dream Maze and Walk-In Dome. It is possible to stay dry while passing through these fountains, but expect your children to get soaked. Some visitors say the Magic Water Circuit is more impressive than the Bellagio fountains in Las Vegas.

Adjacent to the National Stadium between the Via Expresa and Arequipa Avenue, Parque de la Reserva is located just south of the historic city center on the northern border of Lince. If you go at about 6 p.m., just before sunset, you can see the fountains in both the daylight and the dark. At 7:15, 8:15, and 9:30 is the Fantasy Fountain Show, a water-and-laser-light show set to music.

6. HUACA PUCLLANA

Huaca Pucllana
Cl. General Borgoño s/n, Miraflores
Hours: 9 a.m. to 5 p.m. Closed Tuesdays.
Admission: 12 soles ($3)
huacapucllanamiraflores.pe

Huaca Pucllana, also known as Huaca Juliana, is the best-restored of Lima's many archaeological sites. It is also the most convenient to visit given its location in Miraflores, which lends an interesting contrast of an ancient civilization surrounded by the heights of modernity.

Built by the Lima Culture in 200 A.D., the adobe-and-clay pyramid served as an important ceremonial temple and administrative center for the various cultures which prospered in the Lima region before the arrival of the Spanish conquistadors.

Visitors must take a guided tour, available in English, which explains how pre-Columbian cultures survived in this desert. Mannequins illustrate how the people made bricks out of the sand.

The Lima Culture built canals redirecting water from the three main rivers to irrigate the entire valley. A small nursery shows which crops and livestock the civilizations raised in Lima, but fish would have been these cultures' primary source of protein.

The intricate brickwork of the pyramid comes alive with tasteful illumination at night. Night tours are available Tuesdays through Sundays from 7 p.m. to 10 p.m. There's also an on-site restaurant which offers diners the chance to look out over the ruins while they eat.

Huaca Pucllana is our recommended archaeological activity because its Miraflores location makes it the most accessible and it would not take an entire day. But anthropology and archaeology enthusiasts will be more interested in

Pachacamac, an hour south of central Lima. The oracle which sits on top of Pachacamac made it the most important holy site in the region for more than 1,000 years. The adobe complex is several times the size of Huaca Pucllana.

Those hardcore archaeology aficionados may want to make the trip to Caral-Supe, the oldest city in the Americas five hours north of Lima. Caral would require staying overnight.

For those looking for something shorter than the guided tour at Huaca Pucllana, Huaca Huallamarca in San Isidro is conveniently located and can be seen in under an hour with no guide. Also known as "Pan de Azucar" (Sugar Loaf).

7. PARAGLIDING

Parapuerto
Parque del Amor, Miraflores
Hours: 10 a.m. to 6 p.m.
Price: 260 soles ($80)
www.parapuerto.com

Spend any length of time in Miraflores and you'll inevitably notice paragliders swooping up and down the Costa Verde, and even buzzing past Larcomar's restaurants at lunchtime. Taking to the air gives a quick thrill and the best view in all of Lima.

Most of the views from high vantage points in Lima are less than inspiring. From Cerro San Cristobal downtown, you see a flat, sprawled city with few interesting landmarks, rendered even duller by the ubiquitous gray and brown. The views above Arco Morisco at Parque de la Amistad and the hillside slums during a shantytown tour are even less interesting.

Paragliding over Miraflores gives a bird's eye view of the sea, green cliffs and the modern, upscale apartment towers of Miraflores, Barranco and San Isidro. It is inarguably the best view in Lima, albeit an expensive one.

I am not at all an adventure junkie or extreme-sport enthusiast, and the ride itself wasn't too intense for me. Unless you have a paralyzing fear of heights, don't be afraid of paragliding. The moderate thrill it gives does not come from an adrenaline rush so much as the beautiful, 360-degree view.

The takeoff point is located in a grassy field in the Malecon boardwalk between Parque Raimondi and Parque del Amor, a short walk from Larcomar. The 10-minute passenger flights cruise up and down the coast over Miraflores between 230 and 500 feet in altitude.

Many different operators offer passenger flights, but they are all directed through one kiosk managed by Paraport, a private company licensed by the Miraflores district. So you do not have to book a professional beforehand. Just show up at the launching point.

While you do not have to book a flight beforehand, you may want to call Paraport to confirm that weather conditions will allow you to go. When the winds are not strong, the company reduces the weight limit for tandem flights. On normal days, the weight limit is 265 pounds.

But on days with light winds, they can reduce that limit to 180 pounds. A Paraport official told me that on rare cases, winds get so light that they have to reduce the limit to just 110 pounds.

I went on a day when the limit was 180 pounds, and I weigh 230 pounds. Fortunately a lighter instructor (Luis of Fly Adventure) who could take me was working that day. So it's a good idea to call beforehand to confirm wind speeds. They speak English: 970 547 238.

The tandem flights cost 260 soles, or $80, and the guides only accept cash. The price comes with an HD video of the flight, which they give you on a memory card.

Paraport manages the flights, but the guides who take you up in the air are independent operators. Many of them offer discounts if you ask for them by name, so you can save a few soles by searching "Lima paragliding" and contacting them through their websites.

Aeroexteme and PeruFly are two of the more popular companies. Many of them teach classes where you can learn how to paraglide alone, but authorization to fly over the cliffs will likely require an eight- to 10-day course.

The view over Miraflores is best during the summer when the city's not blanketed in fog. But the winter is when the winds are strongest, and the green coast of Miraflores certainly has its charms in cloudy weather.

8. LIMA BIKE TOUR

Cycling is the best way to see a city because you're not passing too fast to see interesting sites, as in a car or bus, and you are not limited to the areas you can walk or run to. On a bicycle, you can cover a lot of territory at a speed that allows you to take in the sights.

Lima is the ideal city for cycling because it never rains, it's flat and there are protected bike paths called "ciclovias." Arequipa Avenue, a major vein stretching from Miraflores to the city center, is closed to cars on Sundays until 1 p.m., during which all four lanes fill with pedestrians, rollerbladers, skateboarders and cyclists. They call the event "ciclodia" (Cycle Day), and it's great for people-watching without the stress of cars and honking horns.

Sunday is the best day to do a Lima bike tour, but any day will do.

On all days besides Sundays, you'll have to ride in the street with traffic. Latin American traffic is different than the United States or northern Europe in that there is less order. It may seem chaotic to the inexperienced eye, but there is a method to the madness. You will pick it up quickly.

Unfortunately however, in my experience Lima's drivers are the least respectful of pedestrians and cyclists compared to other Latin American cities. Remember to ride defensively because the rules of the road here, especially among bus drivers and taxis, are different than the norms you may be used to.

If you want to minimize your exposure to traffic, take a guided bike tour with Bike Tours of Lima (www.biketoursoflima.com). The company also rents bicycles if you'd like to explore on your own. They have high-quality bikes, they're honest and their shop is conveniently located in the heart of Miraflores.

To rent a bike and take a tour without a guide, I have designed a Short (four miles), Medium (8.5 miles) and Long Tour (14 miles), the latter of which spans Miraflores, San Isidro, Lince, downtown, Jesus Maria and Magdalena. Take the Short Tour if you don't want to deal with much traffic. See my tour routes with detailed instructions and custom Google Maps at limacitykings.com/lima-bike-tour.

9. SHANTYTOWN TOUR

Shantytown tours are one of the more recent developments in Lima's tourism scene. While walking tours of the historic city center, Miraflores and Barranco are the heart and soul of Lima tourism, visiting only the upscale areas give a jaded view of the city. For people who want to get off the beaten path, a shantytown tour is an excellent option to see the real Peru.

Known as "pueblos jovenes" in Peruvian Spanish, shantytowns are a common phenomenon across Latin America where inefficient and over-regulating governments cannot accommodate the legal requirements to build housing in societies with high rates of poverty. They are "favelas" in Brazil or "comunas" in Colombia. They were called Hoovervilles in the United States during the Great Depression.

When a family needs some kind of shelter but can't afford to buy an existing home and/or land, the natural recourse is to buy rudimentary construction materials, stake out a piece of unused land and build a place to live. Effectively homemade housing, it's completely illegal and unregulated.

While the phenomenon is seen across Latin America, few cities saw the extent that Lima did. In fact, the majority of Lima's housing today was originally built informally or "extra-legally." In time these neighborhoods acquire electricity, running water, paved roads and even legal title.

The shantytown tours take place in the mountainous desert far from the heart of the city. It's not the most beautiful land even in the summer months. In the winter, it's foggy desert. The original shantytowns were built in the valleys, but nonstop immigration to the capital has pushed development onto the hillsides. The further from the city and the higher up the mountains you go, the deeper the poverty. Any shantytown tour will require lots of climbing stairs.

There are several Shantytown Tour operators, but the original is Haku Tours (www.hakutours.com). Founder Edwin Rojas grew up in Villa el Salvador before it had running water. He tells what it was like to fetch buckets from Chorrillos hours away. As a child he knew Villa El Salvador's most famous resident, Maria Elena Moyano, whose 1992 assassination by the Shining Path outraged the nation. Edwin uses 100% percent of the revenue from his shantytown tours to build daycare centers, schools and soup kitchens in the area. So if you take the Lima Reality Tour with Haku Tours, all of your money will support the local residents.

10. GASTRONOMY

At the time of this writing, Peru has won five consecutive World Travel Awards for best culinary destination. Lima is one of the world's best cities for gastronomy and food tourism. Peruvian food is unlike any other in its inventiveness and creativity. Here are the most important dishes to try while in Lima.

To see a photo album of these dishes and more, visit goo.gl/PuatQM.

Ceviche

Peru's signature dish is raw fish marinated in lime juice, which kills the bacteria. The fish is served with sweet potato, red onion, white corn, seaweed and fresh "rocoto," a Peruvian spicy pepper. The lime is sour, the sweet potato is sweet, the rocoto is spicy and all three combine for a Holy Trinity of flavor.

Ceviche is a healthy plate to boot. Raw fish is loaded with Omega-3 fatty acids and protein. Lime juice adds your recommended daily intake of Vitamin C. Sweet potatoes are so low on the glycemic index they're almost not a starch. Corn and onion pack a little fiber, and seaweed is one of the most vitamin-dense foods on the planet.

One quirk the nutrition-conscious may want to be aware of with ceviche is "glaceado" sweet potato, in which the sweet potato is drizzled in simple syrup to make it sweeter. It's too sweet for some, including me. You'll know glazed sweet potato because it's shiny. But I've found perfection in restaurants which use just a touch of orange juice on the sweet potato.

Ceviche is often served with beer. "Cevicheria" is a ceviche restaurant, but in parts of Lima it's almost synonymous with "bar," so you're likely to try your ceviche in the middle of a daytime drinking scene.

If you don't want raw fish, "ceviche de mariscos" is shellfish ceviche. The shellfish is fully cooked before being marinated in lime juice. If you're willing to eat just a little raw fish but not an entire plate, "ceviche mixto" has both cooked shellfish and raw fish.

The "leche de tigre" (tiger's milk) is the fishy lime juice at the bottom of the bowl. Cevicherias offer a shot glass of it a la carte. I like to mix it with beer.

Ceviche restaurants would be called "seafood restaurants" in English, since most serve a selection of cooked-fish dishes. Arroz con Mariscos (seafood with rice) and Picante de Mariscos (a spicier version) are mainstays, along with "Chicharron" (fried fish), soups, stews and more. So you don't have to eat raw fish at the cevicherias.

Aji de Gallina

Aji de Gallina is usually the Peruvian favorite in the hearts of tourists who don't dig ceviche. Aji de Gallina is shredded chicken breast tossed in a mild yellow-pepper-and-peanut sauce with rice. The sauce is made with evaporated milk, yellow aji peppers, Parmesan cheese, garlic, onion and crushed peanuts or pecans. Boiled eggs, potatoes and black olives are served with the chicken and rice. This is Dave's favorite.

Aji de Gallina is one of four dishes that typically come with a Piqueo Criollo, or Creole combo platter. The others are Carapulcra, Cau Cau (tripe stew) and beans.

Arroz con Pato

Arroz con Pato, or "rice with duck," is the signature dish of the northern city of Chiclayo. But like many of Peru's regional dishes, it has conquered Lima and become a mainstay in the national cuisine.

More commonly found with chicken as Arroz con Pollo, the recipe calls for enough cilantro to turn the rice bright green. Chicken or duck legs and thighs with steamed peas and carrots top the cilantro-infused rice and red pepper, with tomato and onion on the side.

Every country in Latin America has its own version of Arroz con Pollo – rice with chicken. Peru's is the best.

Causa Limeña

This signature Lima dish is a mashed-potato cake filled with chicken or tuna salad and avocado. Causa is basically a chicken-salad sandwich with mashed potato instead of bread. Yellow potato is mashed with lime juice, yellow aji and olive oil. It's a filling dish, often served in small portions as an appetizer.

Chicken or tuna causa are the most common, but Lima's ceviche restaurants serve other variants and inventions which are too numerous to list here. Two of the most common include orange causa made with spicy rocoto and crabmeat and purple causa made with black olives and octopus. Above is a trilogy of inventive causas courtesy of La Choza Nautica in Breña.

"Causa" is a popular slang term unique to Lima, meaning "dude" or "mate." If you want to sound like you live here, you can greet people with "¿Qué tal, causa?"

Lomo Saltado

Peru's most popular dish among less experimental eaters, Lomo Saltado contains strips of sirloin, tomato and onion cooked in soy sauce, tossed with fried potatoes and rice and topped with fresh parsley.

Peruvian steak and fries. Anything ending with "Saltado" will be cooked in soy sauce with tomatoes and onions and served with fries. Pollo Saltado, Tallarin Saltado, etc.

Lomo Saltado was inspired by Chifa, the Chinese-Peruvian fusion created by Lima's Chinese community.

Tacu Tacu

Another Lima specialty is the Afro-Peruvian creation, Tacu Tacu. Garbanzo beans or lentils are mashed with rice, onion, garlic and yellow aji pepper, formed into a mold and fried. The Tacu Tacu is served alongside beef, fish or any other kind of meat. Sometimes topped with fried egg and plantain.

Ceviche is Colin's favorite plate in Peruvian cuisine, but his favorite dish in Lima is a Tacu Tacu variant served at El Rincon Que No Conoces in Lince. Their "Tacu Tere," named for the late chef, Teresa Izquierdo, is Tacu Tacu stuffed with beef or pork tenderloin and served with fried tomato and onion with chorizo, fried egg and plantain. The flavor contrasts are guaranteed to please.

Another winning combination is Tacu Tacu with Lomo Saltado, in which the latter's juice is the perfect complement for the mold.

Seco de Cordero

Seco de Cordero is lamb stewed in a cilantro-onion-garlic sauce served with rice and garbanzo beans. Seco de Res uses the same ingredients with beef in place of lamb – usually a rump roast cut – and is what you'll find at the cheap restaurants. Seco de Cabra, which you'll most likely find at Chiclayo-style restaurants, uses goat meat.

Seco de Cordero is the most visible evidence of the Moorish legacy in Spanish Peru. The dish is a Peruvianized version of the Moroccan dish, Lamb Tagine.

Carapulcra

Tacu Tacu is one contribution, but the signature Afro-Peruvian food is Carapulcra. This pork dish hails from Chincha Alta, the historic Afro-Peruvian city in the department of Ica, just south of Lima. The tangy sauce is made with paprika, yellow aji pepper, peanuts, vinegar, white wine, garlic and other spices.

Carapulcra is often served with Sopa Seca instead of rice. Sopa Seca is the hometown plate of Cañete, another Afro-Peruvian town on the southern coast of Lima department near the border with Ica, not far from Chincha Alta. While it translates to "dry soup," Sopa Seca is super-salty pasta cooked in chicken, basil and parsley.

Carapulcra with rice is excellent, but it is best served with Sopa Seca. Carapulcra is one of four dishes that typically come with a Piqueo Criollo, or Creole combo platter. The others are Aji de Gallina, Cau Cau (tripe stew) and beans.

Sangrecita

Sangrecita is similar to "black pudding" or "blood sausage" in Europe, or "morcilla" elsewhere in Latin America. Cooked chicken blood flavored with garlic, onion and spicy rocoto is served with rice or other starches as seen above.

The iron-heavy flavor is definitely an acquired taste, especially for Americans who have no equivalent. But I have certainly acquired the taste to the point where I get regular cravings.

Like Arroz con Pato and Seco de Cordero, Sangrecita is another contribution from northern Peru. Restaurants specializing in Trujillo, Chiclayo or Piura cuisine will be the best places to eat Sangrecita.

Chifa

You can't go far in Lima without passing a chifa restaurant. In Barrio Chino and parts of Lince, you will see roasted ducks hanging in storefront windows. The best ones are in Lima's Chinatown (featured in the Downtown Lima Walking Tour). If you like Chinese food, you should try the Peruvian fusion.

Like Chinese restaurants around the world, some are fast and cheap while others are fine dining. While there are too many dishes to name here, some plates are found everywhere.

Chaufa is fried rice. Pollo Enrollado is a battered and fried tube of chicken breast served with veggies and rice which, along with Pollo Chijuakai (sesame chicken), are recommended for those who don't like sweet sauces. Pollo Tipakay (sweet and sour chicken) and Chancho con Tamarindo (pineapple pork) are sweet staples at Chifa restaurants.

In Latin America, lunch is the most important meal, as opposed to the United States and Northern Europe where dinner is considered more important. So most typical Peruvian foods are not served at night, unless of course you're in the tourist districts where restaurants cater to people from the United States and northern Europe.

Outside of Miraflores, however, the dining options narrow significantly after 4 p.m. Chifa is one of the cuisines open for dinner, usually until late. Another typical dinner is Anticuchos.

Anticuchos

Anticuchos, the typical late-night food in Lima, are barbecued beef hearts served with boiled or fried potatoes. Don't be afraid, the cow heart is rather lean. Many tourists who try Anticuchos have no idea they're eating hearts. It's like a tough steak.

Alongside the beef hearts, traditional Anticucho restaurants also serve Mollejitas (chicken gizzards) and Panza (beef tripe). I was not a fan of either gizzards or tripe back in the States, but the Anticucho marinade has converted me so now I always order a combo platter featuring all three. Again, I have acquired the taste and sometimes get cravings.

For you party animals, Anticucho restaurants are the most common establishments to be open after midnight.

Sandwich de Chicharron

A wildly popular staple, albeit lesser known on the world stage, is the Lima-style fried-pork sandwich. Slices of pork fried in lard are topped with fried sweet potato slices and salsa criolla (red onion doused in salt, lime juice and a touch of spicy rocoto pepper).

While you can find the Chicharron Sandwich both day and night, they are often a breakfast food for Saturday and Sunday mornings. Great nourishment to help cope with that hangover.

The venerable El Chinito chain is an icon in Lima known for having the best Chicharron Sandwiches in town (pictured above), offering delivery in the upscale districts.

While Chicharron Sandwich is inarguably the sandwich champion of the City of Kings, it only recently won over Lima's hearts and minds. The more traditional Lima sandwich was the Butifarra, which features Peruvian-style ham, lettuce, "salsa criolla" (onion-pepper relish with lime and cilantro) and mayonnaise on French bread. Sometimes listed as "Jamon del Pais," El Chinito serves a killer Butifarra as well.

Papa a la Huancaina

Papa a la Huancaina is an appetizer of boiled potato covered in a mildly spicy, cheesy cream sauce. As indicated in the name, the dish was created in Huancayo, the provincial capital of the Junin department which sits at over 10,000 feet in altitude in the Andes Mountains.

Papa a la Huancaina is one of few dishes from the Andean highlands to catch on and become ubiquitous in Lima. Unlike Arroz con Pato and Carapulcra, however, Papa a la Huancaina may be more common in Lima than in its hometown. Like Causa, it's served cold, which probably explains why it is so popular in Lima's sweltering summer.

Suspiro de Limeña

Suspiro de Limeña, or Lima Woman's Sigh, is a parfait made of condensed milk, eggs, and sweet-red-wine meringue. It's served in tiny portions because it's so sweet that just a little will more than satisfy your sweet tooth.

Despite being named after the city of Lima, Suspiro de Limeña can be difficult to find outside the tourist districts. It's not a great seller among Lima's residents, whose palates must have moved away from such rich sweets since this delicacy was popularized in the colonial era. But you should not have trouble finding it at tourist restaurants, especially near the always dependable Parque Kennedy.

Picarones

Suspiro de Limeña may be the namesake, but by popularity Picarones are the undisputed champion of Lima desserts. The fried doughnuts drenched in fig honey are another throwback to Arabic cuisine and the Moorish legacy in colonial Spain.

Unlike Suspiro de Limeña, you'll be able to find Picarones almost anywhere. They are commonly sold by street vendors in parks and always at festivals. The purple Picarones are infused with purple corn, which barely affects the flavor. The Picarones pictured above were served at Jose Antonio, whose notable fig flavor makes their Picarones syrup unrivaled.

Chicha Morada

Chicha Morada is a juice made by boiling purple corn, pineapple and apple, then adding lime, sugar and cinnamon. It is unbelievably refreshing in the summer, making it Lima's signature noncarbonated beverage.

There may be an obscure brand or two which are tolerable, but in general do not buy bottled Chicha Morada. It must be homemade! If lemonade always tasted like the Minute Maid version, it never would have become so cherished in the southern United States.

Inca Kola

Peru's plutonium-colored soda, Inca Kola, tastes like bubblegum. Started by a British family in the 1930s, the brand is now an icon and source of pride throughout Peru.

Inca Kola is unique in being one of a few soft drinks in the world which outsells the world's bestseller, Coca-Cola, in its home market. In other words, Peruvians drink more Inca Kola than Coca-Cola, so you'll have a hard time getting out of Peru without trying it.

Inca Kola was so successful that Coca-Cola bought it outright. Today Inca Kola is distributed throughout the United States and much of Europe at boutique import groceries.

Pisco Sour

Peru's national liquor, pisco, is a spirit distilled from grapes. It can be rather harsh for the first time, especially the cheaper brands. The more expensive brands, however, are smoother and gaining traction in the global market.

Bar Maury, pictured above, invented the Pisco Sour in the early 1900s when an American guest asked for a whiskey sour, but the bartender had no whiskey.

Pisco Sours are made by blending pisco with ice, simple syrup, lime juice and an egg white. They are sweet and foamy. But don't think this sugary, frozen drink is "girly." They are stronger than they taste, and if you don't be careful they'll put you on the floor. I have typically masculine tastes in almost exclusively drinking beer, sometimes punctuated with shots of whiskey. And I'll go for a night of Pisco Sours once in a while.

Many cocktail bars serve variations like the Maracuya Sour and Chicha Sour with passionfruit juice or Chicha Morada in place of lime. If you'd like something sweeter and not so strong, try an Algarrobina, which mixes pisco with black carob syrup and evaporated milk to make a cocktail similar to a chocolate martini.

If you can't see yourself drinking a frozen drink with sugar all night, the top pisco cocktail for binge drinkers is the Chilcano – pisco with ginger ale and lime. Teenagers, amateurs and street drinkers mix pisco with Sprite.

Chapter 11
Restaurants

As Peruvian food has recently grown in international popularity, Lima has established itself as a top culinary destination. In 2016 Lima laid claim to three of Latin America's 10 best restaurants, including #1 and #2, and nine of the top 50.

Lima's restaurant scene is the best in Latin America, offering everything from set lunches for $3 to multi-course tasting menus for $100.

For the budget-conscious, the best way to get the most food for your sol is to look for the mom-and-pop restaurants known as "menus." These places are easy to find, so we don't list them here. Set lunches normally include a soup to start, an entree of meat (chicken, fish, beef, or pork) and rice and a glass of juice. The food is cheap and fast.

Serious foodies and those looking to splurge will find most of Lima's notable restaurants listed below. However, you don't have to go to any of them to eat great food in Lima. There are great restaurants in every neighborhood, and only a phone book could list them all.

Something about Western culture has trained North Americans and Europeans to look for that one special restaurant where you have to order this or that plate you can't get anywhere else. But in Latin America, it's more important to eat the traditional plates. So focus on the dishes listed in the previous chapter at any neighborhood restaurant, and you'll be fine.

In fact, you can't really get traditional Peruvian food at many of the "best" restaurants as defined by a Pellegrino-sponsored British magazine which anointed itself the world's authority. The food at those places is definitely good, but much of it is a celebrity chef's invention as opposed to traditional Peruvian cuisine.

Bottom line, you don't have to eat at any of the restaurants listed below to get great Peruvian food.

PERUVIAN

La Rosa Nautica
Espigon 4 Circuito de Playas, Miraflores
$$

It's impossible not to notice La Rosa Nautica, pictured above, when looking out over the Pacific Ocean from the cliffs of Miraflores. This Lima icon is located at the end of a wooden pier out at sea, giving it a unique atmosphere with waves splashing against the pylons below and surfers in the surrounding waters.

Due to its popularity with tourists and tour groups, it's best to make a reservation if you want to go for lunch or dinner. There's also a popular bar if you're only looking for a drink.

Astrid & Gaston
Av. Paz Soldan 290, San Isidro
$$$

After training in Spain and France, celebrity chef Gaston Acurio returned to Lima in 1994 and, with his wife Astrid, opened Astrid & Gaston. Today Acurio is one of the world's top chefs with restaurants around the world and credited with helping to bring Peruvian cuisine to the forefront. In 2013, Astrid & Gaston was recognized as the best restaurant in Latin America and #14 in the world.

Ayahuasca Restobar Lounge
Av. San Martin 130, Barranco
$$

The colorful and artsy Ayahuasca bar is housed in a 120-year-old mansion in bohemian Barranco. Its owners specifically set out to create an atmosphere that breaks from the routine, yet remains warm and inviting.

Ayahuasca takes its name from a hallucinogenic drink traditionally taken by indigenous tribes in the Amazon rain forest. At night Ayahuasca is a popular cocktail lounge.

Cafe de la Paz
Cl. Lima 365, Miraflores
$$

Located in Parque Kennedy, Cafe de la Paz is a comfortable and convenient spot to sample classic renditions of Peruvian cuisine, including at night. The outdoor seating is perfect for people watching. Dave recommends Causa Limeña as well as the Club de la Paz sandwich.

Central Restaurante
Cl. Santa Isabel 376, Miraflores
$$$

Chef Virgilio Martinez started out studying law before switching to the culinary arts. Trained at Le Cordon Bleu in London with culinary experience around the world, Martinez returned to Lima to open Central. The restaurant has since surpassed Astrid y Gaston according to the restaurant-rankers to be the best in Peru.

The appetizer list alone is enough to entice seafood lovers with spicy ceviche, octopus, mussels, shrimp and tuna. Meat lovers can opt for the beef carpaccio with foie gras, and there are several desserts to choose from as well.

Chifa San Joy Lao
Jr. Ucayali 779, Cercado
Av. Caminos del Inca 1899 in Surco
$$

Chifa is ubiquitous throughout Lima, but the fine-dining restaurants are not. Founded in 1927, San Joy Lao is the Chinese-Peruvian flagship in downtown Lima's Barrio Chino. Another high-end Chifa option with a buffet is Restaurante Royal in San Isidro.

El Bolivariano
Pasaje Santa Rosa 291, Pueblo Libre
$$

El Bolivariano serves up traditional Peruvian food in a 230-year-old house just one block from Pueblo Libre's Plaza Bolivar square. On Sundays El Bolivariano serves an excellent buffet which makes it the best option for those looking to taste several traditional dishes in one sitting.

El Bolivariano produced the Lomo Saltado and Aji de Gallina dishes featured in the Gastronomy section of this guide.

Another option for a Peruvian-cuisine buffet is the Rustica chain.

El Rincon Que No Conoces
Cl. Bernardo Alcedo 363, Lince
$$

El Rincon Que No Conoces is the restaurant of the late Teresa Izquierdo, the honored icon of Afro-Peruvian cooking. The Tacu Tere named for her is the Tacu

Tacu creation mentioned in this book's Gastronomy section, and only served on weekends. El Rincon Que No Conoces has a buffet every Wednesday.

Fiesta Chiclayo Gourmet
Av. Reducto 1278, Miraflores
$$$

The northern city of Chiclayo is one of Peru's culinary giants, home to Arroz con Pato and Seco de Cabra (stewed goat). Fiesta's dedication to the regional cuisine of northern Peru has helped set it apart from the many other high-end Peruvian restaurants in Miraflores and won it regional recommendation from world tourism magazines.

Jose Antonio
Jr. Bernardo Monteagudo 200, San Isidro
$$$

Founded in 1972, Jose Antonio is an old standby for Lima's elite to enjoy Creole cuisine. Unlike other high-end restaurants, Jose Antonio does not serve creative inventions by celebrity chefs. It specializes in impeccably prepared, traditional Peruvian cuisine. If you want the most authentic gastronomical experience in Lima, you can't go wrong with Jose Antonio. The building is a relic to the colonial era. The former stable house now adorns religious paintings alongside bull heads and horse saddles. Jose Antonio has two more locations in San Borja and the Asia beach town.

La Choza Nautica
Jr. Breña 204, Breña
Jr. Brigadier Pumacahua 2374, Lince
$$

This cevicheria chain has offered more than 100 different seafood dishes for over 20 years. The strictly middle-class restaurant did not have any locations in the typical tourist areas until the recent opening of a location in Barranco.

The Breña location is just outside the city center, a block from Plaza Bolognesi. The Lince location features live music and often charges a cover on weekend afternoons. There are two more locations in San Miguel and Santa Anita.

La Choza Nautica prepared the Ceviche and Trilogy of Causas pictured in the Gastronomy section.

La Mar Cebicheria
Av. La Mar 770, Miraflores
$$

Gaston Acurio's signature seafood restaurant features eight different types of

ceviche as well as a tasting option. There's much more than ceviche, suc
sushi rolls and rice or pasta dishes. But La Mar doesn't take reservatic
often packed, so be prepared to wait in line.

Acurio has since gone on to open seven other La Mar restaurants around the
world, including San Francisco, Sao Paolo and Bogota.

Las Brujas de Cachiche
Cl. Bolognesi 472, Miraflores
$$$

Las Brujas de Cachiche is another Lima institution. The atmosphere on the
restaurant's main floor is warm and inviting. An open kitchen lets nearby patrons
see in on the culinary action. The restaurant features a 1,500-bottle wine cellar,
which is available for private dinner parties.

On the second floor is Huaringas, a dimly-lit bar where you can nibble on
classic Peruvian finger foods or taste a variety of Pisco Sours. It's the perfect place
to take a date or relax with friends.

This Lima brand has expanded to new locations in Santiago, Bogota, Cartagena,
Panama City and more.

Malabar
Av. Camino Real 101, San Isidro
$$$

Opened in 2004, Malabar sets itself apart from the other fine-dining restaurants
by sourcing unique ingredients from the Peruvian Amazon. It is now ranked
among the top 10 restaurants in Latin America.

If you can't decide what to order, try a little of everything with the seven-course
menu or the nine-course vegetarian tasting.

Panchita
Cl. 2 de Mayo 298, Miraflores
$$$

Opened by Gaston Acurio in 2009, Panchita is known for its huge portions of
traditional Peruvian dishes. The Gastronomy section's picture of Arroz con Pato
was taken at Panchita, and David could only finish half of the plate.

Pescados Capitales
Av. Mariscal La Mar 1337, Miraflores
Av. Primavera 1067, San Borja
$$$

Pescados Capitales is the most popular ceviche and seafood restaurant among
Peruvians, which is to say no celebrity chef or hype. But when locals who have a bit

of money want ceviche, they go here. The name is a play on the words, "pecados capitales," or "deadly sins."

Rafael
Cl. San Martin 300, Miraflores
$$$

Serving modern Peruvian food and named after celebrity chef Rafael Osterling, this restaurant is located in a bright red, 1920s-era home. The interior decor is minimal, yet the walls are adorned with Osterling's personal collection of modern art. In 2013, Rafael was ranked #13 in Latin America.

Restaurante Bar Cordano
Jr. Ancash 202, Cercado
$$

Bar Cordano was opened in downtown Lima by Italian immigrants in 1905. It has since become downtown Lima's best-known restaurant. National politicians and celebrities alike dine and pose for photos.

All of Cordano's Peruvian plates are good, but their signature plate is the Tacu Tacu con Bistec, a huge portion of Tacu Tacu with breaded steak. This plate is pictured with the Tacu Tacu description in the Gastronomy section.

T'anta
Many locations
$$

T'anta is a restaurant chain by Gaston Acurio priced for the middle class. The many locations are comfortable and casual. T'anta offers traditional Peruvian dishes as well as unique creations from the man himself.

Tio Mario
Paseo Chabuca Granda, Barranco
$$

Tio Mario is the best place to try Anticuchos. And if you're not up for cow hearts, get a Lomo platter (steak dinner) for a moderate price. This is also a great place to try Lima's two best desserts, Suspiro de Limeña and Picarones. Located next to Barranco's Puente de Suspiros, Tio Mario is open until 2 a.m.

The photo of Anticuchos in the Gastronomy section was taken at Tio Mario.

INTERNATIONAL

La Bonbonniere
Various locations
$$

La Bonbonniere is a chain of French restaurants established in San Isidro in 1953. If looking for something other than Peruvian in Lima, the vast majority of international restaurants serve American or Italian cuisine. So La Bonbonniere offers Steak Tartare, Chicken in Sauce Verte, French toast for breakfast and of course croissants.

The company has four locations in Lima.

Blue Moon
Jr. Brigadier Mateo Pumacahua 2520, Lince
$$

Blue Moon is an Italian-Peruvian icon serving old-world plates since 1966. The daily buffet features Peruvian seafood alongside Italian pastas, risottos and meats until 5 p.m. The restaurant makes its own Italian-style cold cuts, cheeses, antipastos and chocolates.

The Sicilian-born founder Santino Balleta, who is still there every day, has a passion for game meats including deer, pheasant, rabbit and quail. The deer with green-pepper sauce and vegetable risotto will change your mind about deer.

Como Agua Para Chocolate
Pancho Fierro 108, San Isidro
$

There are many Mexican restaurants throughout Peru, but the vast majority of them do not serve corn tortillas. That detail alone should spell the state of affairs. Como Agua Para Chocolate is the exception which serves authentic Mexican fare and margaritas in San Isidro.

La Bodega de la Trattoria
Various locations
$$

Bodega is one of Lima's most popular Italian restaurants among the moneyed classes, with six locations in the tourist beat. Founded in 1985, the managing company also operates three other Italian-cuisine chains, the finest of which is La Trattoria di Mambrino.

Maido
Cl. San Martin 399, San Isidro
$$$

Ranked second in Latin America in 2016, Maido is the restaurant of chef Mitsuharu Tsumura. His specialty is Nikkei, the Japanese-Peruvian fusion cuisine, as well as traditional Japanese and sushi.

Mantra
Alfredo Benavides 1761, Miraflores
$$

Mantra is the token Indian restaurant in Lima. It certainly won't compare to what you can get in London, but it was good enough to be featured at Mistura in 2016.

Restaurante Rigoletto
Cl. Colon 161-C, Miraflores
$$

Restaurante Rigoletto offers Italian and Mediterranean fusion dishes, as well as classic pastas and risottos. The Peruvian owners cut their teeth in the fine-dining scene of Miami.

Tarboush
Av. Oscar R. Benavides 358, Miraflores
$

Opened in 2000 by a Palestinian immigrant, Tarboush is Lima's best place for authentic Middle Eastern cuisine. Located across the street from Parque Kennedy.

VEGETARIAN

AlmaZen
Cl. General Recavarren 298, Miraflores
$

Located near Parque Kennedy, AlmaZen receives rave reviews from travelers for its fresh, locally-sourced organic foods.

Sabor y Vida
Cl. General Recavarren 156, Miraflores
$

Open for breakfast and lunch, Sabor y Vida's set lunch for 10 soles ($4) is a steal.

COMFORT FOOD

When it's time for a break from the highly experimental Peruvian cuisine, check out these options for familiar foods. But before leaving the Peru universe, there are three options of Peruvian food that even the pickiest eaters will enjoy.

Papa Rellena

Papa Rellena, or stuffed potato, is mashed potato is stuffed with ground beef, seasonings and black olives, formed into a ball, fried and served with spicy aji sauce.

Pollo a la Brasa

Invented by Swiss immigrants to Lima in the 1950s, Pollo a la Brasa is Peruvian-style rotisserie chicken. While Peruvian, roasted chicken is relatively standard fare anybody would like. Served with french fries and a small salad. Chains like Pardo's and Norky's are clean, corporate options on the high end. There are cheaper, independent operations in every neighborhood throughout the city.

Salchipapa

Reportedly invented on the streets of Lima, this Latin American mainstay is simply french fries topped with a chopped hot dog. Peruvians cover Salchipapa with ketchup, mustard, mayonnaise and spicy aji sauce. Some fast-food stands offer egg or shredded chicken on top as well.

Manolo
Av. Larco 608, Miraflores
$

Founded in 1968, Manolo is a safe sandwich shop a block south of Parque Kennedy. They offer sandwiches of turkey, pork, roast beef, ham, chicken and more served with fries. It's a great place to try the Butifarra. Manolo also serves pizzas, pastas and more with fresh juices, coffee, hot chocolate and other beverages. Manolo is known for its churros, a traditional Spanish dessert.

Osso
Calle Tahiti 175, La Molina
$$$

Peruvian chef Renzo Garibaldi studied international business in Miami before working as a chef for Gaston Acurio in San Francisco, where he discovered and fell in love with the American-style steaks. He realized there was nowhere to get a fat, bloody steak in Lima, so he opened a proper American steakhouse in the upscale district of La Molina. He is now known in Peru as "the meat prophet," and Osso is a Michelin 3-star restaurant.

Wingman
Av. Miguel Grau 188, Barranco
$$

Unfortunately there is no place in Lima to get slow-smoked, St. Louis-style BBQ ribs – my wife's favorite American food. But her second favorite is Buffalo wings, which I can make at home or get at the local Chili's. But when we want the best wings in town, we go to Wingman in Barranco. Another great place for wings – and just a block away – is Barranco Beer Company.

Tres Cuartos Burger Bar
Calle Enrique Palacios 1072, Miraflores
$$

There are many Peruvian-owned restaurants serving up proper American hamburgers. But Tres Cuartos has the most legitimate claim to being the best in Lima.

Tony Roma's
Jockey Plaza, Surco
$$

If you don't want to give Peruvian restaurants serving American food a shot, you don't need a travel guide to help you find the closest McDonald's, KFC, Papa John's or TGI Friday's. But the best American chain restaurant in Lima is Tony Roma's. Classic American fare including BBQ ribs, thick steaks, grilled fish, meal-sized salads, hearty sandwiches and burgers. Jockey Plaza is also home to Lima's Hard Rock Cafe.

Lima Delivery
Mobile app
$

When in doubt, the Lima Delivery app is an easy default to choose food based on restaurants which will deliver to your location. The options change depending on the neighborhood, but you'll always have ample gringo cuisine in the heart of the city.

Chapter 12
Nightlife

Lima's nightlife is one of the city's strong suits, and there is no shortage of neighborhoods packed with bars and clubs where you can drink and dance the night away. As a rule of thumb, the farther from Miraflores and Barranco you go, the less likely you'll be around other foreigners.

Dress codes apply to a small minority of high-end clubs. Men almost never need to worry about dressing up for a night of partying. Jeans and a stylish T-shirt with sneakers are fine.

Peruvian women, however, take greater care with their appearance and are likely to dress nicer than the men. Many Peruvian women won't go grocery shopping without makeup and heels. While foreign women can always get away with wearing jeans and a simple top at the club, keep in mind it's difficult for a woman to be overdressed.

The majority of bars and dance clubs play what's known as "crossover," in which the DJ mixes Latin genres of salsa, reggaeton and cumbia with top 40 hits in English. This variety is appreciated by most Peruvians.

Throughout Latin America, dancing is central to nightlife and dating. Take a few salsa lessons to learn the Latin beats, or just to meet new people. Private lessons cost 30 to 42 soles ($9 to $12) per hour. Peruvians are polite and most will dance when invited.

Many dance clubs "card" patrons, so always bring photo identification or a printed copy of the information page in your passport.

Karaoke is wildly popular in Peru. The karaoke bars are usually expensive and offer formal service. Be forewarned, however, that the talent level of some karaoke bars is so high that the less practiced singers might get booed off the mic. The Sopranos karaoke chain is the most reliable place to find a drinking-and-singing party. Rustica is another option.

Casinos are also common in every neighborhood. Most Peruvians play slot machines, but you can find serious poker in the Miraflores casinos. Atlantic City Casino is the favorite for sports betting on NFL every Sunday.

The bars in Lima stop serving alcohol around 3 a.m. After-hours bars for the hardcore partiers in Lince at Arequipa and Risso avenues.

NIGHTCLUBS AND DANCING

Aura
Larcomar shopping center, Miraflores

Aura (pictured) is a large, modern dance club which attracts a young, upper-class crowd Thursdays, Fridays and Saturdays. The cover charge is 50 soles ($15) per person, making it one of the most expensive dance clubs in Lima. If you want a table, you'll need to make a reservation.

Bizarro Bar
Cl. Francisco De Paula Camino 220, Miraflores

Bizarro Bar first opened in 1992, giving locals a place to go and hear the emerging genres of grunge and electronica. Open Wednesday through Saturday nights in the heart of Miraflores, Bizarro hosts live music as well as Peruvian and foreign DJ's.

El Bolivariano
Pasaje Santa Rosa 291, Pueblo Libre

Our recommended buffet for Peruvian cuisine converts its large space into a dance club and bar at night for a more mature crowd. The restaurant is big enough to usually accommodate dancing and tables for everybody.

El Dragon de Barranco
Av. Nicolas de Pierola 168, Barranco

This dance club is open most nights of the week and is especially popular on Wednesdays. The music varies nightly. Popular with foreigners as well as Peruvians.

Gotica
Larcomar shopping center, Miraflores.

This high-end dance club is a mainstay among Lima's hottest places to see and be seen.

La Noche
Av. Bolognesi 307, Barranco

Part bar, part cultural center, La Noche offers live concerts among other events throughout the week. Arrive early on the weekends to ensure a seat. Mondays are popular for jazz.

Pub Cubano
Cl. San Martin 443, Miraflores

Cuban-style salsa bar. Check the website for information on dance classes.

Rustica
Multiple locations throughout Lima

A buffet by day, a bar and dance club for a mature and middle-class crowd by night with locations throughout the city. Rustica is a good option for less serious karaoke.

Son de Cuba
Calle de las Pizzas, Miraflores

Salsa bar with classes located in Miraflores's Calle de las Pizzas.

Tumbao VIP Miraflores
Cl. Bellavista 237, Miraflores

This chain of dance clubs was started by Vernis Hernandez, a Cuban salsa singer who immigrated to Peru. The Miraflores location behind Calle de las Pizzas is a dependable, large club for live salsa bands and crossover music. Their location on the beach south of Lima is popular during summer weekends.

BARS

Bar Maury
Jr. Ucayali 201, Cercado

Bar Maury is the hotel bar one block south of Plaza de Armas which invented the pisco sour. Bartenders in bow ties work behind an elegant oak bar under giant paintings depicting Peruvian Creole culture. Bar Maury is a regular setting in "Conversation in the Cathedral," Mario Vargas Llosa's classic novel set in 1950s Lima.

Bar Queirolo
Jr. Camana 900, Cercado

One block southwest of Plaza San Martin, Bar Queirolo is Lima's oldest bar. Queirolo is a national pisco and wine brand in Peru. You can sample their portfolio by the bottle or glass. It's a great place for a group of friends to sit down with a bottle of liquor. Queirolo also serves good food, with a full lunch menu. At night they offer a pared-down list of hot plates, plus sandwiches and a variety of cheese, olive and salami combinations.

Calle de las Pizzas
El Paseo San Ramon, Miraflores

This small pedestrian alley runs between Diagonal and Bellavista and is easy to see from Parque Kennedy. Filled with pizza shops offering mediocre food, hostesses entice diners with a free glass of wine or pisco sour. There are several bars and dance clubs. It's worth a visit if you're short on time in the city, but once is enough. Watch out for pickpockets, prostitutes and the pepera women who drug your drink.

The Corner Bar and Grill
Av. Larco 1207, Miraflores

You don't have to watch soccer when you have The Corner, the American expat community's bar of choice to watch NFL, MLB, NBA, NHL, NCAA, UFC and boxing. Food is mediocre at best but they're sure to have the game.

Capitan Melendez
Cl. Alcanfores 199, Miraflores

Capitan Melendez is a small, pisco-themed bar in Miraflores. If you're looking for an old-school, no-frills place to sample various pisco sours, give the Capitan a try.

Gran Hotel Bolivar
Jr. de la Union 958, Cercado

This hotel ironically faces Plaza San Martin, named for Jose de San Martin, who ultimately became something of a nemesis to Simon Bolivar. Gran Hotel Bolivar is a Lima landmark and probably its most famous bar. The signature drink, La Catedral, is an oversized pisco sour.

Prices are on the expensive side for the downtown area. Some of the clientele wear suits and ties. There is a nice smoking patio overlooking La Colmena.

Huaringas Bar
Cl. Bolognesi 472, Miraflores

This three-level bar is attached to the popular restaurant, Las Brujas de Cachiche. The first level is a typical bar, while the second and third levels are small, comfortable lounges. The upper levels are the perfect place to take a date after dinner, or for a drink before going out dancing.

La Calesa
Cl. Miguel Bañon 255, San Isidro

This elegant and smoke-free bar with comfortable sofas and tables offers an amazing array of infused piscos. Dozens of Peruvian herbs and spices can be found infused into pisco. If you chat up the bartender, he'll serve you free samples. La Calesa draws an older and upper-class crowd. A friend once saw Gaston Acurio stumbling out.

Om Bar Lounge
Cl. San Martin 400, Miraflores

An old, non-descript house converted into a lounge. Better for grabbing a drink and chatting with friends than dancing. Popular on Tuesday nights in addition to weekends.

Munich Bar
Jr. Union 1044, Cercado

This basement bar is one of few in Lima to serve draft beer. And keeping with the German theme, the draft beer is served in ceramic beer steins. The bar features a piano and serves what is recognized as the best salchipapa in Peru. Bar Munich's version features five kinds of sausages, including a white weisswurst.

Murphy's Irish Pub
Cl. Schell 619, Miraflores

Murphy's is Lima's top Irish pub and host to the city's best St. Patrick's Day party. It's more of a live-music venue than an Irish bar, however. You may not see any rugby or hurling matches on TV, but you can catch Conor McGregor's next fight.

Picas
Bajada de Baños 340, Barranco

Restaurant, bar and lounge next to the Puente de Suspiros landmark in

Barranco, a short walk uphill from the sea.

Taberna Queirolo
General Manuel Vivanco, Pueblo Libre

Located on the opposite side of the same square block as El Bolivariano in Plaza Bolivar is Taberna Queirolo, a second location for the Queirolo brand with the same concept as Bar Queirolo downtown, albeit a little finer. On weekends, get a table early or you won't get one.

Chapter 13
Parks and Plazas

In Latin America, parks and plazas are a central part of life. Instead of back yards, people go to public spaces to be outdoors with family, friends or significant others.

PUBLIC SQUARES

The central plaza is less of a place to bring the dog and have a picnic in the grass than a place to see and be seen on a park bench surrounded by restaurants, cafes and other diversions.

Plaza de Armas

Lima's Plaza de Armas, also called Plaza Mayor, is home to the Cathedral of Lima, the Archbishop's Palace, the Government Palace and the Municipal Palace of Lima (city hall).

Soldiers in dress uniform stand guard in front of the Government Palace, which sits far behind iron gates. Francisco Pizarro lived on this same lot, although in a different building, and was assassinated here in the country's first coup d'etat. The colony was subsequently governed by viceroys who resided here, and it is now the official residence of the president of Peru.

The Cathedral of Lima was built to convey the power of the Church in the lives of colonists and natives. The cathedral's museum showcases one of the city's best collections of religious artwork.

The neo-colonial building with the carved wooden balcony is the Archbishop's Palace. In Peru's first century as a Spanish colony, the clergy were reluctant to venture out of the urban centers to preach to the masses of indigenous Peruvians, preferring to stay inside their urban enclaves and service the Spanish elite. In the 17th century, however, the Church put a new focus on conversion, mandating clergy to speak Quechua or Aymara. Converting the former Inca colonies to Christianity was a massive endeavor planned from this palace.

The Municipal Palace of Lima, or city hall, features both the original Charter of Lima signed by Francisco Pizarro and the national Declaration of Independence, but the building is not open to the public.

Bus tours of the historic city center leave from the south side of this plaza every half hour or so. Look for long red buses.

In this plaza you can also catch a bus to the top of Cerro San Cristobal, the highest point in Lima with a panoramic view of the city. But the view isn't the best. A cable car is currently under construction, and has been for years. Another way to visit is by hiring a taxi.

Northwest of the Government Palace is Casa de Aliaga, a colonial-style house preserved by the Aliaga family for hundreds of years. In fact, it claims to be the oldest home in all the Americas. You must make reservations in advance at casadealiaga.com.

Plaza San Martin

Plaza San Martin was named for Jose de San Martin, the Argentine military general who officially declared Peruvian independence on July 28, 1821. Although Simon Bolivar cemented Peruvian independence, he overstayed his welcome and is thus held in less esteem than San Martin, who is displayed on horseback in the magnificent statue in the center of this plaza. The white, baroque architecture and fountain give an effect of grandeur.

For most of the 20th century, Plaza San Martin was the commercial center of downtown Lima. In recent decades, however, it has been relegated to tourism and hosting large protests. Most of downtown Lima's bars are within a block or two from Plaza San Martin.

Alameda Chabuca Granda

Alameda Chabuca Granda is a pedestrian strip behind the Government Palace featuring street entertainment and snacks. In these blocks you'll find storytellers and dancers performing in small amphitheaters. There is also a reasonably priced, outdoor restaurant offering many of Peru's signature dishes.

The flagship monument is a red statue of a woman dancing. The woman is Chabuca Granda, Peru's famous 20th century singer for whom this area is named.

Parque Universitario and Plaza de la Cultura

This dual plaza is separated by La Colmena, the common name for Nicolas de Pierola Avenue, at Abancay Avenue. Overlooking Culture Plaza is the Sacred Heart of Jesus Church. Founded in 1642, the church is more commonly known as Iglesia de los Huerfanos because it was built on the site of an old orphanage.

On the south side of La Colmena is the fenced-in University Park. El Panteon de los Proceres is a museum housing the remains of several Peruvian war heroes, including two-term President Ramon Castilla, who freed the slaves of Peru.

At the east end of University Park is a small amphitheater, where a performing-arts school often puts on traditional dances.

Parque Kennedy

Parque Kennedy is what most people call the central park of Lima at Larco and Jose Pardo avenues, but the official names of the six-acre park also include Parque Central and Parque 7 de Junio.

The focal point of tourism in greater Lima, Parque Kennedy boasts beautiful gardens and ample seating. Its location in the heart of Miraflores makes it a popular gathering point day and night. There is always some kind of street entertainment in daylight hours and early evening. Peruvian artists sell paintings and handicrafts. The area is surrounded by restaurants and bars.

Parque Kennedy is famous for its cats. In the 1980s, the park was infested with rats. Local legend says that the Iglesia Matriz Virgen Milagrosa church adopted a group of cats to combat the rat problem. The story goes that they let the cats prowl the area, and while the rats disappeared, the cat population exploded.

Every few years the city tries to give the cats away in adoption drives, but they're still there today.

Parque Municipal de Barranco

The plaza at the heart of Barranco features the municipal library, the Iglesia de la Santisima Cruz (Church of the Blessed Cross) and several fountains with park benches. It's one block from the Puente de Suspiros bridge and La Ermita chapel. Looking east from the plaza (if you're facing the church, look to your right), you'll see a pedestrian alley. This is Boulevard Sanchez Carrion, a strip of bars and nightclubs.

The Municipal Park of Barranco is located between Pedro de Osma and Miguel Grau avenues in the heart of Barranco.

Plaza Bolivar of Pueblo Libre

The central plaza of Pueblo Libre is home to the National Museum of Archaeology, Anthropology and History. Two blocks east is a military barracks with an aviation display in the front lawn. A short walk away is the Larco Museum, and all around are some of the city's most authentic Peruvian restaurants and bars.

Plaza Bolivar of Pueblo Libre is located on General Manuel Vivanco just west of Brasil Avenue.

Plaza de Armas de Surco

The Plaza de Armas de Surco, also referred to as Plaza Mayor de Surco, is the main square in Surco. It features the 16th-century church, Iglesia Santiago Apostol. The plaza is also the site of the Festival de la Vendimia, Lima's annual wine-and-pisco festival.

GREEN SPACES

When the concrete jungle of Lima has you yearning for some nature, pay a visit to one of these grassy parks.

Malecon

The Malecon is a six-mile strip of parks, gardens and green space along the cliffs overlooking the sea. The pathways are used for biking, rollerblading, skateboarding and jogging. Couples and families lounge in the grass. Others gaze at the sea.

In addition to gardens and ocean views, certain areas offer exercise opportunities with pull-up and dip bars, skateboarding parks and soccer courts. The fitness centers begin after Parque del Amor.

The Malecon is Lima's best park to see and be seen.

Malecon is located on the cliffs above the Pacific Ocean, stretching from Miraflores all the way to Callao, although the entire stretch is not continuous. A Lima must-see, the Malecon is featured in both the Lima Bike Tour and Miraflores Walking Tour.

Parque de la Exposicion

Exhibition Park was built in the 19th century to host the International Exhibition, a modest World's Fair showcasing Peruvian progress. The park is a popular gathering place among university students and home to the MALI Lima Art Museum, the Metropolitan Museum of Lima, a drama school, historic pavilions and statues, a man-made lake and more.

Parque de la Exposicion is located just south of the city center, wedged between Via Expresa and Arequipa Avenue on the east and west, and Paseo Colon and 28 de Julio on the north and south.

Parque de la Reserva

Home to the Magic Water Circuit, Parque de la Reserva was named for the reservists who organized to resist the Chileans during the War of the Pacific in the late 19th century. The park features magnificent fountains and structures adorning Greek columns.

Parque de la Reserva is located a few blocks south of Parque de la Exposicion, between Via Expresa and Avenue Arequipa on the east and west, and Estadio Nacional (National Stadium) and the border of Lince to the north and south.

Parque de la Reserva is downtown Lima's cleanest urban park. It stays that way by limiting its opening hours to before 10 a.m. After that, you will have to visit during the Magic Water Circuit or a special event such as Independence Day celebrations.

Campo de Marte

Campo de Marte is a great park for sports. In addition to the ever-present soccer, you can find basketball and volleyball games. Peru's national swimmers and water-polo team train in the Olympic-sized swimming pool. There is a popular skateboarding park with ramps and half pipes, as well as amphitheaters for dance teams. On weekends the park is packed with families showing their kids the fun of bumper cars and giant, inflated slides.

The park features a famous memorial to Peru's war with Ecuador in 1941, the first of three territorial disputes. There is also a monument to Peru's victims of terrorism and various dedications to the Japanese-Peruvian community, which originally made its home in Jesus Maria.

Campo de Marte is located in the northern tip of Jesus Maria, a block west of Parque de la Exposicion where Salaverry Avenue meets 28 de Julio.

Parque del Amor

Parque del Amor, the Park of Love, features one of the city's landmarks and the Malecon's best-known statue, "El Beso" (The Kiss). The couple kissing in embrace was built by Peruvian sculptor Victor Delfin, who was inspired by a visit to the site with former Lima mayor Alberto Andrade. A couple was kissing and they jumped, ashamed, when they saw the two men. In those times, public displays of affection were scandalous in Peru.

Deflin told the couple not to worry, and at that moment he and the mayor decided to make a safe haven for public displays of affection. Built in 1993, the piece was initially controversial.

Parque del Amor is located within the Malecon along the seaside cliffs, a short walk from Larcomar or Parque Kennedy. Just beyond Parque del Amor is the La Marina lighthouse. Built in 1900, "El Faro" is another Lima landmark.

Parque de la Amistad

Friendship Park is a giant green space in Surco known for the Arco Morisco, or Moorish Arch, a gift from Spain. You can see for miles around from its towers on a clear day. The park has an antique steam train you can purchase tickets for and ride around the park, which is great for children. Finally, you can navigate a man-made lake on paddleboats. Plenty of traditional treats are available as well as restaurants in this family-friendly park.

Parque de la Amistad is located in Surco at the corner of Caminos del Inca Avenue and Nazarenas Street.

Parque El Olivar

In the 16th century a Spanish colonist brought several olive trees from Seville to Peru, but only three of them survived the trip. He planted those three in an area outside Lima near the Huatica River. Over 250 years later, there were almost 3,000 olive trees.

In 1959, Peru declared the 24-acre El Olivar forest a cultural heritage site. Today Parque El Olivar is one of Lima's largest green spaces and home to the El Olivar cultural center as well as over 15 species of birds.

Commonly known as "El Bosque," Olive Grove Park is a clean, green island nestled in a quiet, upscale neighborhood of San Isidro. There isn't much in the way of activities – no sports, playgrounds or dance teams – which is the attraction, a quiet getaway from the crowds in a city where tranquility is hard to find. The affluence of the surrounding homes makes Parque El Olivar one of greater Lima's most beautiful areas.

Parque El Olivar is located just west of where Arequipa Avenue meets Santa Cruz Avenue in San Isidro.

Parque Mariscal Ramon Castilla

Parque Castilla, commonly known as "Touring" for the old driver's-license testing center across the street, is a popular park in Lince with a children's playground, video games, go-carts, a man-made pond with paddleboats and fish-feeding, an exercise center where a bodyweight community trains and amphitheaters for choreography teams. The dance teams were recently banned but that won't likely last by the time you read this.

On the other side of Cesar Vallejo Avenue from all that stuff is a half-mile track which circles small woods where families bring their dogs. The huge trees provide much-needed shade for runners in the summertime.

Parque Castilla is located in Lince on Cesar Vallejo Avenue, a few blocks west of Arequipa Avenue.

Parque Ecologico Loma Amarilla

Yellow Hill Ecological Park is a 19-acre green space sometimes referred to as "the lungs of Surco." Where nearby Parque de la Amistad offers children's entertainment, Loma Amarilla provides a brief respite from the chaos of the city. The park is home to 34 species of birds and 23 species of trees, navigated by a popular jogging track.

Chapter 14
Family-Friendly Lima

The first edition of this guide did not have a family-friendly chapter. But now that I have two children and one on the way, I'm more aware of parents' needs.

MAGIC WATER CIRCUIT

Far and away, second to none, the most fun for children in Lima is the Magic Water Circuit. This is one of our top 10 recommended activities in Lima with or without children. But the ability to get wet makes it that much more fun.

The Magic Water Circuit is located downtown in Parque de la Reserva, sometimes called "Parque de Aguas." While this is better in the hot summer months, it is open in the winter.

For pictures, video and maps, visit limacitykings.com/magic-water-circuit-parque-reserva.

PARQUE DE LAS LEYENDAS

Parque de las Leyendas, or Legends Park, was built on a pre-Columbian huaca. The space is now home to Lima's zoo. There are also small museums and an archaeological exhibit showcasing the Lima Culture.

To be honest, this zoo isn't going to impress anybody from the United States. But it's not bad on Latin American standards, and it makes this list because it isn't just a zoo. There is a giant playground with free and premium rides, which makes it more of a permanent carnival. A grass auditorium regularly hosts live music and other entertainment for children. And some of the animal exhibits – especially those from the Amazon rainforest – are truly unique.

Parque de las Leyendas is also home to the Maranga archaeological site, a small complex of huacas with pictures depicting life before the Spaniards.

Parque de las Leyendas is located in San Miguel, just west of Pueblo Libre and the country's most prestigious university, Peru's Catholic University. The park is on the west side of Jose de la Riva Aguero and south of Venezuela Avenue.

For pictures, video and maps, visit limacitykings.com/parque-de-las-leyendas-lima-zoo.

PARQUE DE LA AMISTAD

This park mentioned in the previous chapter has a steam train which circumnavigates the park. Train rides are fun for all children, but any devoted fanatic of Thomas and Friends like my boy cannot miss this park. In addition to the train, there are models on display all around the park.

Parque de la Amistad has a playground, but its design makes it a little dangerous for small toddlers. There is also a manmade lake with ducks and paddleboats. The food court is home to excellent restaurants representing most of Peru's regional cuisines, and cart vendors peddle typical Lima sweets.

Admission is free for Parque de la Amistad, located at Benavides Avenue and Caminos del Inca. For maps, pictures and video, visit limacitykings.com/parque-de-la-amistad-surco-lima-peru.

PARQUE DE LA IMAGINACION

Park of Imagination is effectively the Lima science center featuring plenty of interactive exhibits as well as guided workshops. My boy loved to get dressed up in the firefighters' uniform and take a ride around in the fire truck.

There is a train ride through a dinosaur exhibit, an aquarium and several workshops for older children.

Located next door to the Parque de las Leyendas zoo in San Miguel, the $4 admission is a steal.

Parque de la Imaginacion
Av. Jose de la Riva Agüero s/n, San Miguel
Hours: 9 a.m. to 6 p.m.
Admission: 13 soles ($4)
www.elparquedelaimaginacion.com.pe

DIVERCITY

Divercity is a more sophisticated science center and educational experience compared to Parque de la Imaginacion. According to the official website:

Boys and girls between the ages of 3 and 13 can assume role-play from among 45 trades and professions to learn how the real world works. Children can realize their dream of being a doctor, firefighter, pilot, factory worker and many more. They can make decisions and take on challenges while learning in a fun way within a city made for them.

Where this concept may be a little too advanced for small children, it would be more fun for boys and girls over 10 years old than Parque de la Imaginacion.

Divercity
Jockey Plaza, Surco
Closed Mondays
Admission: 48.50 soles ($14) for children, 23 soles ($7) for adults
www.divercity.com.pe

Chapter 15
Lima Pueblos

Lima's beach season runs from January through mid-April. But the beaches in the city are rocky and the water isn't the cleanest. For a better experience you need to head south.

In the winter from June to September, the thing to do is escape the dense fog covering the city to find some sun. That means getting to the other side of the Andes Mountains.

BEACH TOWNS

Private buses known as "colectivos" shuttle passengers all day long between Lima and the beach towns south of the city during the summer. You can catch them underneath the bridge at the intersection of Benavides Avenue and the Panamericana Sur highway. Or you can negotiate with a taxi to take you to Asia, Punta Hermosa or San Bartolo.

Asia

During the summer, Lima's hottest nightclubs thin out because all the chic, young and beautiful head to Asia, the hardest partying beach town for Lima's upper classes.

A modern shopping center, Boulevard de Asia, features department stores, popular restaurants and several dance clubs. The beach is a 10-minute walk away. Aquavit Hotel features the hottest pool parties, but you'll need to book at least a few weeks in advance to get a room there.

There's little to no hotel information online, so unless you book a vacation rental from an agency in Lima, you'll have to find a place once you arrive.

Asia is due south on the Pan-American Highway, 90 minutes by car or three hours by bus.

Punta Hermosa

Punta Hermosa is an easy day-trip from the city and features two popular beaches. Playa Silencio (ironically) tends to be more crowded, while Playa Blanca is more exclusive.

Playa Blanca is geared toward the vacation-rental crowd. The boardwalk is lined with homes as opposed to shops and restaurants. Renters are given priority with regard to tents and umbrellas on the beach, but if you go midweek there is plenty of space.

Punta Hermosa features several surf camps (My Surf Camp, Nomadsurfers) and dance clubs. These beachside clubs become popular weekend destinations during the summer.

San Bartolo

San Bartolo is just south of Punta Hermosa. The rough waves beyond a gentle bay make it popular among both surfers and families. There are plenty of hotels in walking distance of the beach, almost none of them online.

Other beach towns south of the city include Santa Maria del Mar, Pucusana, Chilca, San Antonio and too many more to list.

To the north of Lima is Ancon, a formerly exclusive beach town which grew popular among Lima's working classes with Peru's economic growth, prompting the migration of wealthier beachgoers to Asia. The beaches of Ancon are packed during the summer, people on top of people. Ancon is the first of a handful more beaches to the north, all less expensive than the southern beaches.

ESCAPING 'LA GRIS'

While Limeños flock to the beaches outside the city during the summer months, they look to escape the cold, gray skies during winter. To do that, you just need to pass over the closest heights of the Andes Mountains which serve as a barrier for the evaporating clouds from the ocean. Several towns not far from Lima see sunshine all year round thanks to this phenomenon.

Canta

Sixty miles northeast of Lima is the picturesque town of Canta, a favorite weekend getaway for rolling mountains, clear skies and fresh air. After exploring the colonial pueblo, visit nearby Obrajillo to eat the local trout and enjoy the countryside on foot or horseback. Nearby is the Cantamarca archaeological site which dates back to 1100 A.D. Or have a guide take you to Pumacoto ruins, the "Sacred Place of the Puma."

Canta is three hours from Lima by car, but it is not served by the major bus companies. If you do not want to hire a taxi to take you there, which would not be cheap, you can catch colectivo buses to Canta from the Kilometro 22 marker on Tupac Amaru Avenue in the northern district of Carabayllo for 10 to 20 soles ($3 to $6). Lima's hundreds of tourism agencies can take you for guided trips priced in all-inclusive packages.

Cieneguilla

For those who don't want to spend a whole weekend away from the city, the town of Cieneguilla is an easy day trip just beyond the eastern mountains. There are many sunny villages just east of Lima, such as Chosica for example, but Cieneguilla is the nicest and more touristic.

The town has many walled, outdoor restaurants where Lima's middle- and upper-class families flock so the children can run around in the grass, play on playgrounds and trampolines or swim in pools while the adults order food and drinks while watching live music or even Peruvian Paso horse competitions. As in Canta, trout is the thing to eat in Cieneguilla.

If you're feeling more adventurous than a day inside a giant, outdoor restaurant, Cieneguilla tour guides offer hiking, mountain biking and horseback riding packages.

Buses serving Cieneguilla leave from the intersection of Javier Prado and Aviacion avenues in San Borja as well as Javier Prado with La Molina Avenue in La Molina for less than 10 soles ($3). Or you can hire a taxi.

Chapter 16
Beyond Lima

Here are three must-see places in Peru, including one largely overlooked city, with short overviews of the tourist attractions.

MACHU PICCHU
SOUTH AMERICA'S CROWN JEWEL

Cusco is the former capital of the Incas, the largest pre-Columbian empire in the Americas which spanned modern-day Colombia, Ecuador, Peru, Bolivia, Chile and Argentina. Cusco is also the starting point for tourists going to Machu Picchu, South America's crown jewel.

Cusco's elevation is 11,000ft (3,400m), twice as high as Denver. The city boasts 16th-century Spanish architecture and spectacular views of the mountains. Unfortunately the Spanish conquistadors sacked the city during the Conquest of Peru, and in the process demolished most Inca buildings to remove gold adornments. Very little Inca architecture remains.

Machu Picchu

It's unclear whether the first Spaniards knew about Machu Picchu. As I alluded in the first chapter, they probably wouldn't have been interested. The site was forgotten for 400 years until American historian Hiram Bingham discovered it in 1901. Machu Picchu was developed for tourism and now receives over 2,000 visitors per day.

Most visitors take the four-hour train from Cusco to Aguas Calientes, the tiny town at the base of Machu Picchu, and then a bus to the top of the mountain. Trekking enthusiasts pay a premium to take the original Inca Trail, a four-day hike from Cusco which showcases the area's natural beauty before arriving at the majestic apex of the trip. The number of trekkers, guides and porters allowed on the trail each day is limited. If you prefer this option, you'll need to book an all-inclusive trip weeks in advance.

Cusco City Tour

These are some of the top points of interest located in Cusco:
- Santo Domingo Cathedral
- Compañia Church
- Museum of Religious Art (Archbishop's Palace)
- Qoricancha
- Hatun Rumiyoc and the 12-Angle Stone
- Museum of pre-Columbian Art
- Inka Museum

Cristo Blanco and Saksaywaman

On top of a nearby mountain, a White Christ monument overlooks the city. The site can be reached on foot, but it's a steep hike. The climb will take you through interesting Cusco neighborhoods, making it worth the effort. Otherwise, Cusco's many tour agents sell bus tours to Cristo Blanco and Saksaywaman.

Saksaywaman is an awe-inspiring example of Inca architecture. As seen in the Hatun Rumiyoc and the 12-Angle Stone, Inca engineers devised a method of cutting large rocks and giant boulders to fit perfectly. Laborers were drawn from all over the Inca kingdom to build these impressive public works, which baffle today's architects.

Valle Sagrado and Ollantaytambo

Valle Sagrado, or Sacred Valley of the Incas, features breathtaking views of the Andes Mountains and an escape from the noise in Cusco. Because of the massive influx of global tourism, Cusco and Machu Picchu can be overwhelming. In the Valle Sagrado and surrounding pueblos of Chinchero, Pisac, Urubamba, Ollantaytambo and Quillabamba, you can enjoy the picturesque scenery and native Peruvian culture in peace and quiet.

The Sacred Valley is excellent for natural Andean beauty, and the Inca ruins at Ollantaytambo are second only to Machu Picchu.

Party

Two-thousand international tourists enter Machu Picchu each day. There are at least twice as many in Cusco on any given night, making it a small party town unlike any other in Peru. The nightlife never stops. Inside the packed dance clubs, you might not see one Peruvian face, but a global village. Many bars offer free drinks to bring customers in the door.

Gastronomy

There are more than enough restaurants catering to tourists in Cusco. Overall, the food quality is high, whether you're eating a traditional dish from the region or a Western favorite. Dining at the restaurants facing the Plaza de Armas will be more expensive than those a few blocks away, but the views are worth it.

As far as traditional fare, I recommend the Cusco-style Chicharron: thick cuts of pork fried in lard and topped with lime juice, onion and mint leaves, served with fried potatoes and toasted corn. It's the best fried pork plate in the world.

Dave recommends the alpaca steak, a leaner alternative to red meat. You'll find alpaca on many restaurants' menus, each with their own unique spin on sauces and presentation.

Another typical Andean plate is Pachamanca, a combination of various meats such as beef, pork and alpaca with potatoes, cassava and corn cooked in an earthen oven on stones heated by the blazing sun, a more convenient resource than firewood.

AREQUIPA: THE WHITE CITY

Located in the south of the country, Arequipa is Peru's second largest city, three hours from the coast by car. With an altitude of 7,500ft (2,300m), Arequipa is 50 percent higher than Denver.

The historic downtown area was built with sillar, a white volcanic rock which gives the city its nickname, La Ciudad Blanca (The White City). The city is overlooked by Andean peaks of 19,000ft (5,800m), and Arequipeños enjoy a backdrop of snow-capped mountains for much of the year.

Overshadowed by Machu Picchu and Lima, Arequipa often goes unnoticed. But with its own gastronomy that rivals some South American nations, this charming city is sure to please with its distinct architecture, friendly people and mild weather.

Downtown Arequipa Walking Tour

On every block you'll pass centuries-old churches and structures built in the formidable sillar, decorated with intricate stonework. A UNESCO World Heritage Site, Arequipa has strict building codes to preserve the architectural heritage and the city's namesake. The Andean Sanctuaries Museum features the preserved remains of the 400-year-old Inca Ice Maiden, "Juanita."

These points of interest are all easily accessible in a day's walk:

- Plaza de Armas and the Basilica Cathedral
- Andean Sanctuaries Museum
- Casa del Moral
- San Agustin Church
- San Francisco Church

- Plaza España

Monasterio de Santa Catalina

Santa Catalina Monastery was built in the 16th century and takes up two square blocks of downtown Arequipa. Inside is a small town closed off to the outside world. It's a sillar maze of hallways painted in bright blues, oranges and reds leading to courtyards, gardens, fountains, living quarters, dining rooms and kitchens.

The convent's stated mission was to liberate souls stranded in purgatory. Nuns pledged to a life of simplicity in hopes of reaching the highest spiritual level. But it became quite the party house when the nuns had servants, drank wine and were entertained with music. In the 18th century its reputation got so bad the Pope sent a well-known nun to reform Santa Catalina.

Colca Canyon

Colca Canyon is almost twice as deep as the Grand Canyon in the United States, but its fissure shape doesn't look as big. Still, Colca's natural beauty is breathtaking. The Colca Valley and neighboring pueblos make Colca an excellent tourist destination.

At Cruz del Condor, tourists gather to glimpse the Andean Condor, a symbol of pride in South America. The Western Hemisphere's largest flying bird can weigh up to 35 pounds with an average wingspan of 10 feet. The Colca Valley's rolling green hills and mountainside terraces is worth an album of pictures. The Incas built these terraces to increase the surface area available for agriculture and to raise llamas. Canoeing and hiking trips are available for those who want more than a glance of Colca.

Any tour of Colca will bring you to the main squares of pueblos like Chivay, Yanque and Maca, where young girls perform traditional indigenous dances, older women offer pictures with owls and llamas or sell handicrafts. The nearby La Calera Hot Springs are natural, hot-spring swimming pools where servers sell fresh juices, beer and cocktails to swimmers.

Molino de Sabandia

The Sabandia Mill was built in 1621, early in Peru's colonial days. Today, it is a restored farm for tourists offering a look at agriculture 400 years ago, before electricity or the steam engine. The driving force of water is used to power grindstones to make wheat, potato or corn flour.

The mill is built of the quintessential raw material of Arequipa, sillar, and set against the backdrop of green countryside on the banks of a stream. On the mill grounds, visitors watch chickens, ducks, rabbits, guinea pigs, llamas, goats, horses and even bulls. Horseback riding is available. The restaurant next door serves some of the best Arequipa cuisine in the region. Great for children.

Gastronomy

The cuisine of Arequipa is so unique that, in many of the city's restaurants you won't find the Peruvian food in the Gastronomy section of this guide. They only serve Arequipeño, which is good enough to garner entire districts of "picanterias" in Lima. Below are the specialties.

Rocoto Relleno, Arequipa's signature dish, is a spicy pepper stuffed with beef and cheese and served with Pastel de Papa, the local potato casserole. If you have a big appetite, order a Doble, which comes with rocoto relleno, Pastel de Papa and baked or fried pork tenderloin.

Adobo is a tangy pork-chop soup and standalone meal. Only served on Sundays outside the tourist restaurants, Adobo is traditional hangover food. The downtown restaurants start serving it at 4 a.m.

Chupe de Camarones, or Arequipa-style Shrimp Chowder, is excellent but be forewarned: the shrimps come out whole. The shrimp are never shucked or altered before serving in Arequipa. With shrimp or any kind of meat, Arequipeños love to suck the shell, bones, juice, marrow and everything else.

Estofado de Res is a tangy beef stew with rice. Generous portions of roast cuts are stewed with Chicha de Jora juice, carrots, peas, onion, tomato and bay leaves.

Locro de Pecho is beef brisket boiled until soft and mixed in a mildly spicy, mashed-potato sauce and fresh mint leaves.

HUARAZ AND THE CORDILLERA BLANCA

Huaraz, capital of the Ancash region north of Lima, is the gateway to Peru's Cordillera Blanca, the world's highest tropical mountain range. This city of 120,000 people is perched at an elevation of 10,170 feet. The surrounding mountains tower overhead.

While Huaraz is very touristic, this is our off-the-beat destination outside Lima. After Lima, Machu Picchu and Arequipa, the next most popular cities would be a tie between Puno, Trujillo and Iquitos as people seek out indigenous highlands, northern beaches and Amazon ecotourism. With so much to offer, adventure sports in a cold-weather region get lost.

Huaraz is thrilling for exploring the natural beauty of the sierra, which is home to pumas, cordillera hawks, Andean condors and the rare Puya Raimondi plant. Taking its name from Peru's tallest mountain, Huascaran National Park was established in 1975 and later recognized as a UNESCO World Heritage Site in 1985. A personal guide, transportation and admission to the park can be arranged in an all-inclusive package for as little as 70 soles ($20).

Huaraz attracts mountain climbers from around the world, many of whom are looking to attempt peaks like Huascaran, Peru's tallest at 22,205 feet. For those who prefer to stay below the snowline, there are popular day trips and multi-day treks. The Cordillera Blanca offers spectacular views of lakes and glaciers easily accessible for those travelers who are not so keen on intense physical exercise when on vacation.

The easiest way to reach Huaraz is by bus, a seven- to eight-hour ride north of Lima. Allow yourself a few days of rest to acclimate to the altitude. Drink lots of water, get plenty of sleep and limit your alcohol and caffeine intake. Coca tea is a great help for altitude sickness in high-altitude cities like Cusco, Arequipa and Huaraz.

The best time to visit Huaraz is during the dry season between June and

September. Tourism begins to drop off with the start of the wet season in October, and more than a few shops and restaurants close until the following March. Avoid the rainy season which peaks in January and February.

Pastoruri Glacier

Located 16,404 feet above sea level, the Pastoruri Glacier is quickly shrinking due to global warming. Day tours are available for 70 soles ($20) and include transportation, park admission and lunch.

Almost the entire trip is spent in the minivan, except for the short 30- to 40-minute walk between the parking lot and glacier. If you prefer not to walk, which can be difficult due to the altitude, small horses are available for hire.

Chavin de Huantar

Chavin is a UNESCO-listed archaeological site three hours by bus from Huaraz built by the Chavin Culture which developed in the Andes between 900 and 200 B.C. The Chavin empire ruled over Lima. Chavin de Huantar can be visited as part of a single-day, group tour.

Santa Cruz Trek

The three- to four-day, 31-mile Santa Cruz trek is the most popular expedition in the Cordillera Blanca. Despite being an accessible trek for beginners, it's still a challenge due to the altitude. The high pass is Punta Union at 15,617 feet. Guided treks are available in the peak season, after which frequency of departures tapers off.

Huayhuash Trek

Experienced trekkers can test their stamina on the 10- to 14-day Huayhuash Trek south of Huaraz. The Cordillera Huayhuash features 50 peaks, with six of them over 19,865 feet. Most of the trek is at around 13,000 feet, with a few passes reaching 16,000 feet.

Those who dare to take on this adventure will be treated to some of the most breathtaking scenery in South America. It was here in 1985 that one of the most miraculous survival stories in modern mountaineering took place, as told in "Touching the Void" by Joe Simpson.

Laguna 69

The most popular day hike in the Huaraz area is a three-hour drive from the city and features the bright blue Lake 69, surrounded by incredible scenes of snow-capped mountains. The trek features stunning views of Mount Huascaran and Llanganuco Lakes. The hike is of moderate difficulty, but can be challenging for those who haven't adjusted to the altitude.

About the Authors

COLIN POST

Colin Post publishes Peru Reports, Lima City of Kings and Expat Chronicles. He lives with his wife and children in Lima. Colin used to enjoy basketball, strength-training and drinking beer with friends before family life put all of that aside for the next decade or so.

Follow Colin on Twitter @colinpost and the Lima City of Kings Facebook page.

DAVID LEE

David Lee is a travel writer who has visited over 50 countries across six continents. He is the founder and editor of Go Backpacking, one of the world's premier travel blogs, and Travel Blog Success, a community dedicated to teaching travelers how to build high-quality blogs. When he's not traveling or writing, David enjoys salsa dancing, reading and trying new foods.

Follow Dave on Twitter @rtwdave and connect with him on the Facebook page for Go Backpacking.

ACKNOWLEDGEMENTS

Thanks to Ward for some help with Cusco. See his blog, Life in Peru. Also a hat tip to Rex and his English-language newspaper serving Huaraz, The Huaraz Telegraph. Thanks!

75300966R00064

Made in the USA
Columbia, SC
14 August 2017